THE BODY OF BEATRICE

THE BODY OF
BEATRICE

ROBERT POGUE HARRISON

The Johns Hopkins University Press
Baltimore and London

The Johns Hopkins University Press
701 West 40th Street, Baltimore, Maryland 21211
The Johns Hopkins Press Ltd., London

Library of Congress Cataloging-in-Publication Data
Harrison, Robert Pogue.
  The body of Beatrice / Robert Pogue Harrison.
    p.   cm.
  Bibliography: p.
  Includes index.
  ISBN 0-8018-3680-8 (alk. paper)
    1. Dante Alighieri, 1265–1321. Vita nuova. 2. Cavalcanti, Guido,
d. 1300—Criticism and interpretation. 3. Petrarca, Francesco, 1304–1374—
Criticism and interpretation. 4. Italian poetry—To 1400—History and
criticism. I. Title.
PQ4310.V4H37   1988   88-3944
851'.1—dc19   CIP

The paper used in this publication meets the minimum requirements of American
National Standard for Information Sciences—Permanence of Paper for Printed
Library Materials, ANSI Z39.48-1984.

To Rachel Jacoff

Contents

Preface

The Body of Beatrice deals primarily with Dante's *Vita Nuova* and secondarily with the poetics of Guido Cavalcanti and Petrarch. Because these lyricists are too important, too original, and too theoretically interesting to command the attention of specialists alone, the book is addressed both to a specialized audience and to literary critics interested in speculative questions related to lyric and narrative. From the perspective of those speculative questions the *Vita Nuova* remains a privileged work in literary history, for it represents a unique instance in which the combination of lyric poems and narrative prose creates a deep adversity of paradigms whose implicit tensions become the very essence of the work.

In what follows I try to confront the *Vita Nuova* on its own terms and at the same time to avoid the hermeneutic trap of Dantology. The trap is one that Dante himself set up by embedding within his works the hermeneutic guidelines for interpreting them. The history of Dantology has for the most part followed these guidelines in a persistent effort to expose the authorial intent and genius that govern his artifacts. I am concerned less with authorial intent in the *Vita Nuova* and more with disclosing the deeper recesses in which the work takes on a new life of its own: a new life independent of its canonized author.

Acknowledgments

My deepest thanks go to Giuseppe Mazzotta, who taught me much of what I know about medieval literature. I am also indebted to Thomas Sheehan, Milad Doueihi, and my brother Thomas Harrison for their acute critical readings of previous drafts. Special thanks go to Stanford University and my colleagues in Italian for receiving me into their haven of Italian studies. Finally, I would like to thank Eric Halpern and the editorial staff of the Johns Hopkins University Press for the pleasure of working with them on the publication of the book.

Editions and Translations

Citations from the works of Dante, Cavalcanti, and Petrarch are from the following editions:

La Vita Nuova di Dante Alighieri, ed. Michele Barbi (Firenze: R. Bemporad & Figlio, 1932).

La Divina Commedia secondo l'antica vulgata, ed. Giorgio Petrocchi, 4 vols., (Milano: Mondadori, 1966–67).

Convivio, ed. G. Busnelli and G. Vandelli, 2d ed., ed. Antonio Enzo Quaglio, 2 vols. (Firenze: Le Monnier, 1964).

Dante's Lyric Poetry, ed. Kenelm Foster and Patrick Boyde, 2 vols. (Oxford: Oxford University Press, 1967).

The Poetry of Guido Cavalcanti, ed. and trans. Lowry Nelson, Jr. (New York: Garland Publishing, 1986).

Petrarch's Lyric Poems, ed. and trans. Robert Durling (Cambridge: Harvard University Press, 1976).

All English renderings from the *Vita Nuova* and *Convivio* are my own; Roman numerals refer to chapters, and Arabic numerals refer to lines within chapters. For translations of passages from the *Divine Comedy* I have relied on *The Divine Comedy of Dante Alighieri*, trans. Allen Mandelbaum, 3 vols. (Berkeley and Los Angeles: University of California Press, 1980–82). Other translations are from the cited editions.

Citations from St. Thomas Aquinas are based on *S. Thomae Aquinatis: Opera Omnia*, ed. Roberto Busa S. I., 7 vols. (Stuttgart–Bad Cannstatt: Frommann-Holzboog, 1980).

THE BODY OF BEATRICE

Introduction: Critical Differences

The *Vita Nuova* is a deeply enigmatic work. It will, one hopes, appear even more so by the end of this investigation, especially to those who are familiar with it. But to restore to the work its strangeness, its remoteness, its thought-provoking quality, means to emancipate it from the name of its author—the author of the *Divine Comedy*—and to disengage it from the dense foliage of scholarly prose which has accumulated around it over time. Whether this is possible, or whether such a gesture merely adds a fresh layer to the foliage that naturally gathers around a work by Dante, will have to be decided by others. What I offer here is an attempt to rethink an event in literary history— Dante's encounter with Beatrice—and to defamiliarize our perspective on a traditional work.

But to propose a new perspective means not only to disengage but first and foremost to engage the commentary surrounding the *libello*, or "little book," as the author calls it. Throughout my notes I review various scholars' contributions toward our understanding of the *Vita Nuova*, but notes are by nature fragmentary and local. They do not offer a critical panorama, as it were, and it seems indispensable at the outset to provide a brief account of the dominant trends in the scholarship. A preliminary panorama of this sort serves as both an orientation for the reader and an occasion for the author to acknowledge the labor of others which has made his own possible.

The attempt to provide a critical panorama means once again to confront the old and unresolved problem of national traditions in Dante criticism, for we are dealing essentially with two critical paradigms: the Italian and the American. And they are indeed different. It is not accidental that, with the exception of J. E. Shaw, the protagonists of a prolonged controversy about the composition date of *Vita Nuova* have been exclusively Italian scholars. A number of the fundamental elements that distinguish the tenors of American and Italian Dante criticism are revealed in the former's relative indifference toward, and the latter's relative anxieties about, the matter of fact: Did Dante revise the work much later in his life or not?[1] At a remote historic and geographical distance, the American *dantista* tends to admire Dante's works for artistic and almost mechanistic reasons, marveling at them as wondrous products of a prodigious Gothic genius, as artifacts of a technical complexity that never fails to excite a pseudorationalist delight in order and disorder, or as testimonies of some divine geometry. In short, in the United States one tends to read Dante for the autonomous artifactuality of his works, which explains why the integral works— the *Vita Nuova* and the *Commedia*—are so much more favored than the fragmentary, intermediate treatises. Italians, on the other hand, approach Dante's texts as a heritage, or as monuments of a history that calls for reappropriation and transmission. The historicity of Dante's corpus engages the Italians' own sociofactical historicity at some deeper level of their cultural being in the world. The stronger philological strain in Italian scholarship, which at times exasperates a more theoretically oriented American *dantista*, stems from a concern with the *world* disclosed by Dante's works: the world that, through the transmission of tradition, still claims the peninsula as its own. By the term *world* I mean the sum of specific historical, cultural, and literary coordinates which defines a work's rootedness in a determinate or local tradition. One could even call it an ecotradition. It is this world that even the best American critics are quick to bracket in their quest for Dante's universal literature.

Two momentous books on the *Vita Nuova*, one by Charles Singleton and the other by Domenico De Robertis, epitomize these divergent dispositions in the scholarship. Singleton's *Essay on the "Vita Nuova,"* published in 1949, is an allegory of the

American fascination with the artifactuality of Dante's text, an artifactuality that Singleton reconstructs on the basis of the theological doctrines that supposedly structure the text and saturate it with "meaning."[2] Singleton was the first critic truly to totalize the *Vita Nuova* as a phylomorphic microcosm of the great macrocosmic *Commedia*. Not only did he "make sense" of it as the story of the triumph of Christian *caritas* over secular love, but he showed that the work was interpretable through theological superstructures, numerical symmetries, and patterns of deep structural and semiotic order. Ever since then, American critics who have dealt with the early work by and large have followed the example of Singleton's theologizing and artifactualizing approach.

By contrast, De Robertis's *Il libro della "Vita Nuova"* represents an uncompromising philological tour de force.[3] It undertakes an archaeological survey of the historico-literary framework to which the *Vita Nuova* belongs and in which it has come down to us across the centuries. Recovering the specificity of Dante's cultural, social, and intellectual world through his philological hermenuetics, De Robertis reads the work not as an artifact (let alone a theological artifact) but rather as a document of Dante's literary apprenticeship in late-thirteenth-century Florence. What we have here is a testimony of experimentations, of trials and errors, in a poet's engagement with techniques of expression and literary conventions, as well as a testimony of the appropriation and transformation of classical texts—Cicero's *Laelius de Amicitia*, for example.[4] What motivates the author of the *libello* is above all his faith in literature. Thus, the title of De Robertis's study emphasizes the fact of a *book*. As he reminds us in his first chapter, "L'Idea del libro," it is the *first* book in the history of Italian literature.

From the perspective I adopt in this study, the virtue of one paradigm appears as the vice of the other, and vice versa. De Robertis's typically philologico-literary approach represses the theological or proto-theological dimensions of the *libello*, while Singleton's heavy emphasis on the mystical agenda leaves the specifically literary nature of Dante's enterprise largely un-interrogated. *The Body of Beatrice* embodies a critical alternative that lies outside the parameters of these two paradigms. This critical alternative is *not* a synthesis or fusion of the two, but a different approach altogether. I would call it a phenomenological approach if such a term did not require a series of qualifications which would further delay what is essential to the phenomenological project, namely the attempt to go directly "to the thing itself."

What I propose here, then, is not a theoretical elaboration of my own approach, which speaks for itself in the practice, but above all a reassessment of Singleton's reading of the *Vita Nuova*. I say "above all . . . of Singleton's reading" merely because the American audience by and large continues to ignore *Il libro della "Vita Nuova."* By contrast, Singleton's *An Essay on the "Vita Nuova,"* which has kept generations of American readers under the spell of its paradigm, retains an absolute hegemony with regard to American Dante criticism of the *Vita Nuova.* American critics have tried to expand upon, improve upon, dwell upon the Singletonian paradigm, but always from within its parameters, almost as if the *libello* were more a commentary on Singleton's interpretation rather than the other way around. Given the national context and consequences of my own investigation, therefore, I will conclude these introductory considerations by reassessing the Singletonian model to which we are all indebted but which we must finally overcome if we want to liberate the *Vita Nuova* from the model's constraints.

Singleton Revisited   One of Singleton's important contributions to Dante criticism was his programmatic reading of the synergy between theology and artifactuality in the *Commedia.* His (Spitzerian) rule of never losing sight of the whole, or of the particular's relation to the general, countered a neo-Crocean tendency in Italian scholarship to dismember the poem's organic unity and to isolate individual cantos or segments of the poem. In this way he helped provide an alternative to the rigid *Lectura Dantis* convention by reopening a broad hermeneutic circle that always keeps in view the structural and ideological coherence of Dante's artifact. When he turned to the *Vita Nuova*, he brought this same hermeneutic procedure to bear, confident that the early work obeyed the same laws of unity and resolution which govern the mature masterpiece. It is this assumption, which has been shared by most of the post-Singletonian critics in the United States, that stands in need of correction.

As Giuseppe Mazzotta has pointed out, something like a pseudogenre has developed among American Dante scholars who write on the *Vita Nuova*: the "essay."[5] The word *essay* finds its way into the title of American books and monographs on the *Vita Nuova* like a contagious rhetoric of *sprezzatura*.[6] The term would seem to signal a tentative, noncomprehensive approach, but as one reads these "essays" one finds that they in fact propose a totalizing framework for the *libello*. It gradually becomes clear that the term signals not so much an essayistic approach as a rhetorical adequation between the critical enterprise and the "minor" status of the *Vita Nuova* in Dante's corpus. Under the spell of Singleton's hermeneutic tour de force, American scholars continue to turn to the *libello* with the weighty structures of the *Commedia* in mind, and the result is what one might call the "divine commodification" of the text. The text is geometrized, prodigalized, and theologized, and the enfant terrible is called to order with a slight of hand. It is finally quite amazing to see how docile and manageable the work becomes in the hands of the essayists and to witness the theoretical confidence with which they deal with it.

But let us get specific about Singleton's hermeneutics, for the devil is in the detail.

Singleton bases his reading of the *Vita Nuova* on the opening metaphor in chapter I, sometimes called the "proem," which compares the author to a scribe copying and editing the words he finds written in the book of memory. He declares that this metaphor sets up a relationship of alterity between the protagonist and the narrator, the former portrayed by the latter as living through the events that the latter has already experienced and come to terms with through time. Time, therefore, lies at the origin of this differentiated relationship of identity, for by the end of the narrative narrator and protagonist converge and their relationship of alterity gives way to one of identity. It is from the perspective of the *end* of the narrative trajectory that the protagonist can look back on his experiences and understand their true meaning. The retrospective view of the past thus enables the protagonist to become the enlightened narrator who, like a scribe, transcribes the *sentenzia*, or meaning, of what lies behind him in the book of memory.

Time, then, functions as a principle of revelation. The beginning of the narrative is linked to the end, forming a circle of intelligibility in which the meaning of the narrated events stands revealed.[7] Revelation constitutes the true story of the *Vita Nuova* as its protagonist gradually comes to realize that the signs associated with Beatrice concealed a transcendent meaning. At the time he lived through the events, he could not apprehend these signs as signifiers, let alone grasp their signification, but just as time bridges the gap between protagonist and narrator, so too it bridges the gap that separates these signs from their true meaning, closing the hermeneutic circle, as it were. With the circle's closure comes the revelation that Beatrice's appearance on earth was a miracle. Why else would she have been associated with the number nine? Why else would her greeting have possessed such saving power? And why else would her death have been prefigured in oneiric images of Christ on the cross? These signs reveal their true meaning only after Beatrice departs from the world. Her death, therefore, figures as the condition for revelation. In Singleton's words:

> With the death of Beatrice, a circle is closed. We know again what we began by knowing. And we stand at a

point where we can see that the movement along the line of this action is not movement in a single direction. The current is alternating, which is something one had already seen in the figure of a poet-protagonist become two persons according to a situation in time; the one being he who, though ignorant of the end, moves always toward the end; and the other who, knowing the end, is constantly retracing the whole line of events with the new awareness and transcendent understanding which such superior knowledge can give. (P. 25)

The passage contains the essence of Singleton's interpretation, which posits a point of convergence that enables the end of the narrative to circle back to the beginning and to attain closure in the double movement of the "alternating current." The decisive event in this conversion of perspective allowing the protagonist to become the enlightened narrator of his experience is the death of Beatrice. Singleton insists on the "centrality" of Beatrice's death in the narrative, and he is of course right to do so. However, a certain prudence is required with regard to the notion of a center in the *Vita Nuova*. Singleton, for example, claims that the death of Beatrice occurs numerically at the center of the work. To make the case he first must relocate the place of her death in the chapter sequence. It does *not* take place, he argues, in chapter xxviii—the chapter in which Dante declares her dead—but rather in chapter xxiii, where Dante describes a dream and records a poem that prefigure her death. Singleton writes: "And since the poem [which recounts the protagonist's dream] occurs in a chapter twenty-three, and since the last chapter of the *Vita Nuova* is numbered forty-two, the death of Beatrice could hardly be more centrally placed" (p. 7). Even if we bracket the fact that the *libello* has no real numerical center, or that Dante was notoriously exact when he engaged in numerical correspondences, and even if we try to make of mathematics an inexact science, we still cannot take chapter 23 as the numerical center of the work. Dividing 42 chapters by 2, we fall into the interstice between chapter 21 and chapter 22. Either one of these chapters would be vaguely plausible as a numerical center, but one cannot approximate the center of the *Vita Nuova* as chapter 23 without verging on the arbitrary.

Such dubious mathematics extends also to an algorithm of the number nine in relation to the number of visions contained in the work. Singleton stresses that Dante does not use the terms *visione* and *imaginazione* interchangeably. A *visione* antici-pates the future while an *imaginazione* does not. Now, the num-ber nine accompanies every occurrence of a vision in the work with the exception of the *mirabile visione* of the last chapter. Singleton assures us that "this last is the single exception." Fur-thermore, we should not take it into account when we count the total number of visions in the *Vita Nuova*, for to do so would mean that we would arrive at a sum total of four visions. This in turn would mean the destruction of the perfect corre-spondence between number three and number nine. In Single-ton's words: "There are in the *Vita Nuova*, thus, four visions proper. But it seems more significant to see them as three vi-sions plus one" (p. 15). Such arithmetic may seem "more signifi-cant," but does it work?

The fact is that one cannot count the number of visions in the work, at least not in a clear and distinct way, for Singleton's distinction between a *visione* and an *imaginazione* simply cannot be borne out by the text. Consider the famous dream in chap-ter XXIII which foreshadows the death of Beatrice. Singleton counts it as a vision, but Dante never refers to it as a *visione*; on the contrary, he refers to it as an *imaginazione* at least eight times in the text: "E però mi giunse uno sì forte smarrimento, che chiusi li occhi e cominciai a travagliare sì come farnetica persona ed a *imaginare in questo modo*" (4). Further on in the same passage: "*imaginai* alcuno amico che mi venisse a dire" (6); "e non solamente piangea ne la *imaginazione*" (6); "Io *imaginava* di guardare verso il cielo" (7). Further on: "In questa *imagina*-

zione mi giunse tanta umiltade per vedere lei" (9). And a few lines later: "sì forte era la mia *imaginazione* che piangendo incomincai a dire con verace voce" (10). Dante continues: "e conosciuto lo fallace *imaginare*, rispuosi a loro" (15). And in the *divisione*: "ne la prima dico per ordine di questa *imaginazione*" (31). In light of these passages, which he clearly read with care, it is hard to understand how Singleton ever imagined a rigid distinction between *visione* and *imaginazione*.[8]

The pattern continues. For example, Singleton speaks of the "external architecture" implicit in the poem sequence. That sequence is as follows: 10; I; 4; II; 4; III; 10. The Roman numerals stand for the first, second, and third *canzoni*, while the Arabic numerals stand for the number of sonnets and ballads before and after the *canzoni*. As in the case of the visions, the awkward number four crops up here, and once again Singleton suggests that we merely change our way of counting. First we must bracket the first and last poems of the *libello* and put them in a category of their own; then we must string *canzone* II with the four poems on either side of it; then, leaving the first and third *canzoni* alone, we arrive at the following sequence: 1, 9, 1, 9, 1, 9, 1. "In this way," writes Singleton, "the mysterious number nine is more clearly seen to occur three times" (p. 79).

Even if one concedes that the principle of numerical reason plays this game of hide-and-go-seek, a question arises here: is there a poem sequence at all in the *Vita Nuova?* How can we speak of the "external architecture" of such a sequence when Dante gives two versions of a single sonnet (one of them unfinished) or when he includes in the *libello* part of a *canzone* left unfinished or when he includes two discrete stanzas of a *canzone* written for Beatrice's brother? The *Vita Nuova* contains, technically speaking, five *canzoni*, two of them unfinished. In light of these unfinished poems and the abortive beginning of a sonnet—whose incompleteness is troping the *Vita Nuova* as a "whole," so to speak—and in light of the inherent fragmentations that Dante's work dramatizes in this way, can we still speak about a perfected "architecture" in the sequence of poems? In any case, Singleton speaks eloquently:

> This is more than a matter of extrinsic ornament. Here on the surface are ripples and eddies which are all so many signs of what we know already to lie deeper in the current of the action. As such signs, they make their own contribution to what is the principle intention of the whole form of the Book of Memory: the revealing through signs that Beatrice is a miracle, that she is herself a number nine which, like miracles, is the product of three times three. (P. 79)

What this heavy theologizing and rationalizing passes over is the *libello*'s fundamental preoccupation with poetics, with the ontological status of analogy and metaphor, with the search for a literary idiom adequate to Beatrice. For Singleton the triumph of Christian *caritas* resolves the story of this unfinished story and gives the narrator a privileged perspective on the meaning of the events associated with Beatrice. Perhaps the strongest indication of his will to turn the work into an allegory of the revelation of Christian *caritas* is in his reaction to the famous chapter xxv. As we will see later, it is in this most problematic chapter that Dante outlines a poetics, that he proposes a theory of tropes, that he appeals to the (unorthodox) theories of Cavalcanti, and that he gives a genealogy of vernacular poetic composition. But in Singleton's reading, Dante's preoccupations with the poetic act, the mission of poetry as such, vanish in the light of Christian revelation:

> But this is the way of revelation . . . for it is charity that bursts the narrow confines of troubadour love. It is the presence of charity, hidden in the beginning, which demands at a midpoint on the way of progression from love to charity that the God of Love be abolished. . . .
> The definition of love in chapter xxv in terms of

substance and *accident* does not in itself express all this. But it allows for this to become so. . . . When in other parts of this book it is gradually revealed that love of Beatrice is charity, the strategic importance of this definition is that it has allowed for and does not gainsay a love which is revealed to be charity. (P. 75)

After invoking an obscure distinction St. Bernard once made between "substantial" *caritas* and "created" *caritas* to gloss Dante's definition of love in terms of substance and accident—and without recalling the Cavalcantian resonances of this definition—Singleton concludes with the remark: "All this simply means the Christian truth" (p. 76).[9]

There is no reason to belabor our exercise here. What Singleton would have us believe is what the work invites us to question: that the narrator's *post eventum* perspective allows him to see, and as author to transcribe, the meaning of the events associated with Beatrice. Singleton's entire reading rests on the assumption that the *libello* contains a temporal, teleological endpoint that guarantees the closure of the hermeneutic circle. Such an assumption simply cannot stand up to the ambiguities that characterize the work's ending. The most distinctive feature of the *Vita Nuova*, after all, is that its author does not end his narrative but effectively interrupts it with a promise that he will accomplish at a later date what he has not managed to accomplish in the *libello*. A dramatic failure, an avowed authorial inadequacy, haunt the end of this work. It is hard to see what circle gets closed with the death of Beatrice when the narrative follows a linear trajectory that projects the story into a temporal future at the end of the work. It is fair to say that for Singleton the work effectively ends with the death of Beatrice, and that whatever follows this event—the episode of the *donna gentile*, for example—remains by and large superfluous for his interpretation.

If the death of Beatrice is the condition for the narrator's enlightened speech, why, we might ask, does he remain silent about her death? Why does he refuse to talk about it? He tells us quite clearly in chapter xxviii that he has neither the means nor the perspective to do so. Furthermore, why does he remain silent about the "true meaning" of the first vision in chapter iii? Why, finally, does he end or interrupt the *libello* with a vow of authorial silence, a vow to speak no more until he comes into a more adequate language? These deliberate pockets of silence contain the still unfinished story of the *Vita Nuova*, and the death of Beatrice, around which the silence gathers, disrupts the benevolent semiology that Singleton sees arising from it. Far from closing the circle, the death of Beatrice shatters it, forcing a crisis of temporality on the work. The work as a whole extends into the future, and the retrospective gaze of the narrator *does not* see the terminal meaning of the events lived through by the protagonist, for by the end of the work both narrator and protagonist are looking forward, not backward, in time, to an event that they hope will bring closure to the new life. Revelation, which for Singleton has already happened, remains the outstanding possibility of the *Vita Nuova*, beyond the bounds of its narrative and somehow linked to the absent Beatrice.

Having looked at some of the premises of Singleton's reading and the textual distortions to which they may give rise, it seems necessary in closing to insist on one of the virtues of his essay, namely, the manner in which it takes Beatrice utterly seriously and makes her the authentic matter of the work. On the Italian side, with all its emphasis on the literary features of the *libello*, there is a conspicuous tendency, exemplified by De Robertis, to de-dramatize and de-theologize the figure of Beatrice. In its own way this forfeit fails to do justice to the genetic event out of which the work arises, and in its own way De Robertis's heavy and rigid philological manner represents another form of overkill with regard to the *libello*.

There is a quality about De Robertis's study which, for all the study's erudition and painstaking research, remains unpersuasive, or better, which fails to resonate with the spirit of

Dante's "new life." By this I mean De Robertis's relentless academic archaeology of what he takes to be the dense background of allusion in the work. For every episode, literary inscription, or poetic innovation in the *libello*, De Robertis finds a matrix or genesis in some other traditional text, as if the *Vita Nuova* were essentially an experiment in citation and appropriation. What gets lost in De Robertis's wilderness of philology is precisely the visionary impulse of the work—the intense insistence that everything begins miraculously, with the unaccountable presence of Beatrice. De Robertis remains far too casual in his decision to take this merely as a fictional device on a young writer's part, and it remains strange indeed that in a book on the *Vita Nuova* he has almost nothing to say about the active role of Beatrice in Dante's literary experiment.

Singleton's essay, on the other hand, conveys a distinct sympathy with the visionary wonder of Dante's book. In its own visionary enthusiasm, it often sees in the *libello* what it imagines is there, but the irrevocable virtue that redeems its various hallucinations is, in my view, its insistence on the miraculous status of Beatrice. How one chooses to account for that miraculous status is another question, and it is from the perspective of that question that the inquiry must begin.

BEATRICE
ALIVE

1 Dante's Dream

Beatrice is eighteen years old and walking along a street between two women. Dante perceives her as dressed in white: "Questa mirabile donna apparve a me vestita di colore bianchissimo" (III, 1) ["This miraculous lady appeared to me dressed in purest white"]. Beatrice offers a public greeting, inducing a strange state of inebriation in Dante, who had never heard her utter words before. He removes himself from the street to the privacy of his bedroom ("lo solingo luogo d'una mia camera," which recalls the "secretissima camera de lo cuore" that felt the effects of Dante's first vision of the nine-year-old Beatrice in the preceding chapter), and as he thinks about the courteous lady, he falls asleep and has a "marvelous vision": A fiery mist fills his room, through which he discerns the "lord" of love, fearsome in aspect, who declares that he is Dante's master. Of the many words the lord speaks—they are in Latin—only some are comprehensible. In the lord's arms sleeps a woman, naked except for a crimson cloth [uno drappo sanguigno] wrapped loosely around her body. Looking at her intently, Dante recognizes the lady who had greeted him that same day. In one of the lord's hands Dante sees a flaming object, Dante's burning heart ("Vide cor tuum," says the lord). The lord wakes the young woman in his arms and forces her to eat of the heart. She consumes it reluctantly. The lord, who before seemed joyful, now begins to weep bitterly as both he and Beatrice seem to vanish upwards toward the sky.

Recounted in the prose of the third chapter, this dream establishes the visionary tenor of the *Vita Nuova*, occasions its first poem, and introduces a determinate temporal span between the event and its narration. Numerous attempts have been made to uncover its deeper meaning, by both Dante's contemporaries and later readers, but for the most part they remain precisely that: attempts. I devote the next several pages to an interpretation of the dream not only because the dream represents a hermeneutic challenge but because it conceals the genetic secret of Dante's literary career. The oneiric configuration and sequence of events come together or gather around the essence of that tension that binds him to Beatrice and which makes him resolve, by the end of the *Vita Nuova*, to write of her what has never been written of any woman. Ignoring the question of how Dante may or may not have fulfilled that resolution later in his career, I shall be asking what it is about this *woman*— not the divine agent or angel, not the Christ figure, not the number nine—that makes her "miraculous." For in the final analysis, were Beatrice not first and foremost a woman there would be no apparent reason for Dante to insist upon her so-called miraculous status. We must begin, then, with a phenomenology of vision, for Dante *sees* something in or about Beatrice which cannot be explained merely in terms of poetic hyperbole, phantasmal perception, or even mystical delirium. The accretion of poetic and mystical hyperboles around the figure of Beatrice becomes possible only later, for it is Dante's vision or perceptions of her which initiates the poetic enterprise in the first place. Chapter III dramatizes the genetic priority of perception over poetry by recounting how the "marvelous vision" gives rise to the first official poem of Dante's career—"A ciascun' alma presa"—a poem in which he appeals to other poets for help in interpreting the vision's meaning.

To begin with a phenomenology of vision—of the "marvelous vision"—means to interrogate above all the nature of Beatrice's presence, which occasions the vision.[1] We are still very much in the dark when it comes to knowing what was at stake for Dante in Beatrice's presence, for everything about his *libello* and subsequent career urges us to emphasize the fact of her death, her posthumous mummification in paradise. It would almost make sense to speak of her life as merely a precondition for her death. This necrophilia with regard to Beatrice doubtlessly stems from the fact that she had to die in order for Dante's story, as we know it, to get under way or make sense. Her *glory* remains a central element in the theological narrative that goes by the name of Dante, and Beatrice's glory, of course, means her demise and disappearance from the earth.[2] But it is all too easy to overlook the fact that Dante's highly unlikely career received its initial impulse not from Beatrice's death but from the presence that death rendered inaccessible. The *Vita Nuova* offers discrete and even indiscrete insights into what Beatrice's presence entailed for the poet, and even through the visionary mist that surrounds her in the early work, this living Beatrice appears far more persuasive, enigmatic, explosive, than the re-created and cantankerous figure that the *Commedia's* pilgrim will encounter much later in the boisterous processions of the earthly paradise.

Dante scholars would seem not to share this view, for they invariably are in a hurry to rush Beatrice off to her death and glory. The case of Dante's "marvelous vision" represents a typical example of such haste. The overwhelming consensus among commentators is that the vision "foreshadows" Beatrice's death, and that its "meaning" lies therein.[3] But this generic explanation, which has long been taken for granted, neither accounts for the highly specific, idiomorphic symbolism of what Dante sees in his sleep nor distinguishes the meaning of this vision from the others in the *libello* that also foreshadow her death. Some of the questions that remain unanswered are: Who is this lord? Why is Dante's heart burning in the lord's hand? Why is Beatrice, against her will, forced to consume the heart? What does this consumption mean, and why does it bring about a change of disposition in the lord's humor? If the dream harbors some deeper meaning that would explain its figures and narrative logic, that meaning remains concealed. And deliberately so, for an essential dimension of the dream's much-sought-after meaning is its hermeneutic defiance: "Lo verace

giudicio del detto sogno non fue veduto allora per alcuno, ma
ora è manifestissimo a li più semplici" (III, 15) ["The true meaning of this dream was not seen by anyone at the time, but now it
is manifest to even the most simple-minded"]. By making such a
declaration and yet refusing to disclose the dream's "true meaning" for his reader, Dante seems deliberately to have preserved
for us the dream's most essential quality, namely, its hermeneutic provocation.

Some of the responses to the sonnet Dante sent out to the
local versifiers are extant, and we can gauge the vision's hermeneutic challenge by the odd incoherence found in the several
attempts to make sense of it. Cino da Pistoia, a fellow stilnovist,
responded with a sonnet ("Naturalmente chere ogni amadore")
which interprets the lord as an agency of recognition and communication. Love means to show Dante how every lover wants
to make his heart known to his beloved, and he performs the
noble service of communication by feeding the flaming heart to
Beatrice, but in so doing he takes such pity on her that he begins to cry as he vanishes. Cino's logic clearly breaks down before the dream's own logic, for nothing that he postulates con-
ceptually or dogmatically accounts for the vision's culmination
in tears and fear.

The response by Dante da Maiano, a Florentine poet and
physician, is more coherent only to the degree that he refuses to
interpret the vision. In an ironic sonnet ("Di ciò che stato sei
dimandatore"), he advises Dante to wash his testicles with
plenty of water to disperse the noxious vapors that bring on the
delirium of such visions ("che lavi la tua coglia largamente, /
a ciò che stinga e passi lo vapore / lo qual ti fa favoleggiare lo-
quendo"). But by opting for an erotico-phantasmal etiology, da
Maiano merely skirts the challenge of making sense of Dante's
vision.[4]

The response of Guido Cavalcanti deserves particular attention here, if only because it marks the beginning of the notorious friendship that inspired Dante to dedicate his *Vita Nuova*
to this "primo amico." The contradictions and incoherence

that we find in Guido's "explanation" of the vision dramatize not only the vision's opacity but also the pattern of misunderstanding that was to plague the future of this friendship.[5] As De Robertis has remarked, the motif of the heart in love's hand alludes to Guido's own poem "Perchè non fuoro" (*Rime*, XII), which not only pictures Guido's heart in love's hand but also ends with tears and intimations of death. In light of the allusion, the friendship that Dante's sonnet inaugurates between the two poets already contains a prehistory of affiliation.[6] But Guido's sonnet to Dante, "Vedeste, al mio parere," remains problematic, for it represents a deliberate gesture of misunderstanding on Guido's part. Refusing to engage the more sinister and even violent aspects of the dream, it exalts love as a "segnore valente" who presides over the world of honor. One would not expect such an edifying reading from a poet who was committed to a view of the tragic nature of love. By ignoring the darker side of Dante's dream, Guido in effect controverts the Cavalcantianism of Dante's sonnet. His response sends a message of peership to Dante but also weaves a fabric of misunderstanding whose implications will unfold during the course of their friendship.[7]

However that may stand, no one saw the "true meaning" of the dream at the time. We may say, then, that a blind spot lurks at the heart of this visionary experience. The paradox of a visionary blind spot is hinted at by Dante himself, who speaks of the failure "to see" the dream's true meaning ("Lo verace giudicio . . . non fue *veduto*").[8] While Dante suggests that time opens the vision's meaning to full view, after some seven centuries we still are not able to see what he had in mind when he declared as much.[9] Perhaps it is time, then, to bracket the overly hasty conclusion and to ask about the source of the blindness. What is it in the dream that Dante, his fellow poets, and his various critics have so far been unable to see?

The problem has to do with a network of recognitions that take place on that day. The vision follows upon Beatrice's first public recognition of Dante, expressed through her wondrous greeting, her salvific *salute*. In the private phantasmagoria of Dante's room, the words of the lord of love, only partially comprehensible, have to do also with recognition: the lord's identity ("ego dominuus tuus") and Dante's own heart ("Vide cor tuum"). Furthermore, Dante here comes to recognize, after intently scrutinizing her, the woman in love's arms: "Conobbi ch'era la donna de la salute" ["I perceived that she was the lady of the greeting"]. Here we have a reciprocal inscription of recognition by which Dante returns, in some sense, the greeting of Beatrice, for the oneiric recognition that takes place in the room marks the moment of Dante's knowledge that Beatrice is linked to salvation (*salute* in Italian having the double meaning of greeting and saving). The syntax of the phrase "conobbi ch'era la donna de la salute," emphasizing as it does the copula, gives a definitive character to the ontological apprehension that takes place. Beatrice is not only perceived but also recognized as Beatrice.

To be sure, the recognition is problematic enough to coerce into this one moment all the enigmas that run through the *Vita Nuova*. Beatrice here gives herself to perception through a phenomenal guise that reveals and at the same time conceals her nature: she is naked except for a crimson cloth wrapped loosely around her body. The image provokes curiosity much the way the vision as a whole provokes interpretation. Were it not for that one word in the prose, *nuda*, we could never quite be sure of Beatrice's womanhood, her corporeal facticity, as it were. Everywhere else in the *Vita Nuova* she appears only as dressed, that is to say, she appears above all *as* her dress. In chapter ii, for example, when Dante first set eyes on the nine-year-old girl, she was dressed "di nobilissimo colore, umile e sanguigno, cinta e ornata a la guisa che a la sua giovanissima etade convenia" (ii, 4) ["in the most noble of colors, humble and crimson, girded and adorned in the manner appropriate to her young age"]. The perception focuses exclusively upon her attire. In the case of a nine-year-old boy it is, of course, plausible that dress, costume, and color leave the deepest mark in memory, but nine years later, when Dante is at the threshold of manhood and sees Beatrice for the second time, the woman's attire once again completely fills the narrative eye: "Questa mirabile donna apparve a me vestita di colore bianchissimo." Even granting the claims of color symbolism, one must wonder about the psycho-logic that causes the young man's perception to stop once again at the chromatic surface of Beatrice's clothing.[10] Is this a real woman walking on the street or a shrouded phantasm drifting through the merely symbolic space of a poetic imagination?

The "marvelous vision" certifies or vouches for the womanhood of Beatrice by revealing the corporeal density that underlies her dress, or that substantiates her phenomenality. Are we to say, then, that the body of Beatrice is the "repressed" element in Dante's field of vision? An outright psychological or even psychoanalytic reading of the dream, however insightful the results, will not get us very far here. Little psychology is needed to see that the dream entails, among other things, a sexual awakening.[11] The question that a psychoanalytic hermeneutics cannot help us answer is why the psychic pulsations that produce the dream—if we may even call them that—assume this specific and highly charged symbolic configuration. Why does the dream provoke and frustrate hermeneutical desires to unveil its meaning? Where is its blind spot? To ask the question another way: Why is Beatrice's body wrapped in a *drappo sanguigno*, a crimson cloth?

The cloth makes for Beatrice's intangibility even as she lies in love's arms. While it prohibits a view of her naked body, it also allows Dante to recognize the body as a body without violating a code of courtesy to which he was socially and ideologically bound. The cloth, then, acts as a censor, or as a prohibition, but at the same time it acts as the very opposite of this. Insofar as it guards the presence of the naked body by veiling it, the cloth grants Dante the permission to look at the body and to see without seeing, so to speak. It permits such seeing not only in accordance with medieval codes of courtesy but above all in the etymological sense of *per-mittere*: to send through. The veil sends the eye through the veil and allows the body to appear as the image figured by the veil itself. We have here the very genesis of the figure of Beatrice—her poetic potentiality. Beatrice is not the name of an ordinary woman, nor a *senhal* that provides the poet with a set of traditional poetic conventions to imitate, revise, or mannerize. Her name refers to a unique historical experience that exceeds containment by the Provençal and Italian lyric traditions that Dante inherits at the outset of his career. Beatrice means an inaccessible corporeal density made accessible figurally and poetically, or, more broadly speaking, phenomenally. The "marvelous vision" provides a unique insight into the initial impulse of Dante's literary vocation in the way it depicts an originary event of phenomenalization whereby the body of Beatrice gives itself not in itself but in its figurative re-presentation in and through the veil that covers it. In other words, the presence of the *drappo sanguigno* becomes genetic. We may even say that it engenders the presence of every other figure in the dream: the lord of love, for instance, the burning heart, and its consumption. Let us look at these figures.

The lord is a traditional figure, so traditional in fact that he will disappear from the *libello* as soon as Dante's experience takes a dramatic turn into an unprecedented definition of love.[12] We learn later in the narrative that he is nothing more than a prodigious figure of speech, a fictitious personification. Here in the dream, however, he has a role of authority as he literally manipulates the scene of desire: Dante's heart, fraught with phallic symbolism, would consume Beatrice in its fire; but the lord reverses the expectation by handing Beatrice the heart to consume. The fact that a figure of speech, a personification, takes control of the scene and dictates the sequence of events means that the *drappo sanguigno* somehow lies at the origin of the oneiric scene, for the lord's function is ultimately to guard the cloth's concealment of Beatrice's body and to ensure a wholly figurative transaction of desire. Thus, in one of his hands he holds the veiled Beatrice; in the other he holds a flaming emblem of passion. The reversal whereby the erotic or even phallic fire of the heart is consumed by Beatrice figures as a dubious consummation of desire brought on by the lord, for instead of a consummation we have a momentous incorporation of the heart into the withdrawing body of Beatrice.[13]

The flaming heart consumed by Beatrice is a remarkable trope. The heart introduces through metonymy the narrator's presence in the dream. Except for this heart, Dante is altogether absent from the vision. His real presence is as the spectator outside the vision for whom the scene plays itself out. But within the dream, he figures only in and through the emblem of his passion. He sees himself metonymically condensed, as it were, in the figure of a heart burning in the hand of the terrifying lord.[14] His active desire gets reduced to a passive impotence and castrated by the overdetermined circumstance. The flaming object tropologically condenses the raw urgency of desire, but at the same time does it not also represent a sinister fragmentation? The extraction of the lover's heart from his body and the heart's consumption by the beloved is a recurrent motif in medieval literature, found in different versions throughout the *fabliaux* tales, for example, where it usually represents at once a literal dismemberment, a figurative castration, and a metonymic consignment of the dead lover's body to the woman who held it dear.[15] The ruses whereby a jealous husband or rival brings about the heart's consumption constitute a scheme of passionate revenge that presumably reciprocates the trickery of which he deems himself the victim. Essential to the scheme, however, is the macabre literalization of the metaphoric seat of love: the heart itself. Thus extracted, it is reduced to the dead letter of an objectionable passion. But at the same time, such schemes of revenge involve an even more macabre symbolization, in the dead heart, of the castrated phallus of the rival lover. In other words, however great the vengeful impulse to literalize the organ of love and to reduce it to a material consistency that can be consumed, the gesture of extraction seems invariably to fall back into the sphere of the symbolic.

One Dante critic, in his commentary on the "marvelous vision," suggests that we must consider Beatrice's married status, as well as Dante's anxieties about the legitimacy of his love, in this oneiric scene of a terrifying lord, an extracted heart, and a consumption of it by Beatrice amid tears and fears.[16] If we heed Chiappelli's suggestion, as indeed we must, then Dante's dream becomes a literary dream, and one of castration at that. A dream of *his* own death, therefore, and not Beatrice's. Ultimately, as we will see, the "marvelous vision" *is* a dream about the protagonist's finitude more than about Beatrice's, epitomizing the temporal futurity that allows Dante to perceive Beatrice in terms of some transcendent finality. The prophetic quality of vision must be brought back to this dynamic futurity that characterizes the tension that propels Dante toward Beatrice and leads him to suspend the *libello* in a contract with the future. I enlarge upon this dynamic in part 2 of the present study, but without stepping ahead of ourselves here, we see that the literary motif of jealousy and retribution must be inscribed within the logic or outcome of the dream's events. The dream's bizarre figures, in fact its entire drama, forestall an illegitimate act of transgression on Dante's part. The crimson cloth both prohibits and endorses the protagonist's love; and through the agency of the lord, it transfers desire from the sphere of *fol amor* to the legitimate jurisdiction of the poetic. Dante's language for this jurisdiction is that of "the faithful counsel of reason in those things where such counsel is worth heeding." Thus, the lord who holds sway over Dante's love with wise counsel ("nulla volta sofferse che Amore mi reggesse sanza lo fedele consiglio de la ragione" [II, 10]) receives an absolute mandate in the dream to exercise the role of surveillance and injunction.[17] The mandate comes ultimately from the crimson cloth, which enlists the figurative lord to ensure the figurality of love.

The Christological associations of the *drappo sanguigno*

bear expansion here, for the cloth almost certainly alludes to the moment in Revelation when Christ appears to the apostle: "Vestitus erat veste aspersa sanguigno" (19:13). Significantly for our purposes, this image of Christ in a crimson shroud follows immediately after an image of fire: "His eyes were as a flame of fire." Even more significant is the blood in which Christ's shroud has been dipped, making it *sanguigno*.[18] In short, the *sanguigno* color of the cloth obliquely evokes the sacrificial blood of Christ, once offered up as wine to the disciples. Just as the rematerialization of Christ's body and blood in bread and wine represents the founding moment of Christian sacramentality by which the body of Christ maintains its historicity through time, so the crimson cloth wrapped around the body of Beatrice seems to repeat in its own way the moment of sacred metaphor, rendering Beatrice sacramental in nature.

The cloth's color is significant also with regard to its function of censorship, disclosure, and figuration. The *sanguigno* color has a dynamic symbolic role in the *Vita Nuova*. To begin with, it evokes in Dante's personal memory an image of childlike innocence, for Beatrice first appeared to his eyes dressed in the *sanguigno* color: "Apparve vestita di nobilissimo colore . . . sanguigno." In the marvelous vision nine years later, the *drappo sanguigno* reevokes the image of an "angiola giovanissima" adorned with girlish humility and reaffirms Beatrice's modesty in its veiling capacity. Indeed, after Beatrice's death and her gradual passing from Dante's thoughts, this image of the young girl dressed in the *sanguigno* color will overtake the poet's memory and restore her primacy as an agent in Dante's life and destiny. In this respect the *sanguigno* color is one of the great protagonists of what I am tempted to call the "untold" story of the *Vita Nuova*. By the end of the narrative it emerges as the emblem of time and time's thematic continuity in the figure of Beatrice—the emblem, that is, of Dante's narrative itself.

But while it evokes an image of girlish innocence and modesty in Dante's memory, the crimson color also provokes the darker forces of an unconfessed sexuality in the dream, for it would seem to dominate the entire chromatic spectrum of the dream's field of vision. This spectrum consists largely of fire colors. Visually the crimson seems to condense within itself the more diffused hues of orange which we imagine in the fire images: the fire-colored mist as well as Dante's burning heart. The link between *sanguigno* and fire is reinforced by *Purgatorio* XXX, where Beatrice appears to Dante dressed in "color di fiamma" in an overt recall of this moment in the *Vita Nuova*.[19] The chromatic condensation of fire hues in the cloth's color turns the body of Beatrice into a genetic center of imaginary emanations organizing a metaphoric field of desire around itself.

As the lord hands Dante's heart over to Beatrice to consume, the poetic alternative of this new life is assured. The incorporation of the heart marks at once an expropriation and the project of reappropriating Beatrice phenomenally. The incalculable distance between the body of Beatrice and its veil opens the visionary space where a figurative or symbolic order of apperception arises. By preserving or instantiating this distance, the crimson cloth does not lie on Beatrice's body as a specific figure but rather as a metafigure for the source of figuration in its various local forms within the dream. All other oneiric images and events become refractions off the cloth or, better, a symbolic constellation emanating from the supreme centrality of Beatrice's body. In its occultation of the body and its refiguration of it behind the veil and *as* the veil, the cloth in effect generates the dream. As such, the body of Beatrice remains the undisclosed substance of revelation. Its accessibility only through a phenomenal veil binds Dante's new life to the aesthetic order, binds it, in short, to a quest for revelation through the poetic enterprise.

If this much is true, we can see how the dream's blind spot—the veiled body of Beatrice—actually creates the field of vision. The dream's "meaning" remains undisclosed not because it awaits a hermeneutical tour de force that will unlock its secret but because the meaning of the new life has from the beginning been handed over to the body of Beatrice itself, which incorporates desire into the noumenal mysteries that incite desire and bear it into the future.[20]

The correlation I am proposing between the body of Beatrice and *intendimento*, or meaning, is far from impressionistic. As we will see in the chapters that follow, it runs implicitly throughout the *Vita Nuova*. At this point, however, it is necessary to insist that *body* here means more than Beatrice's corporeality. In many instances Beatrice's corporeal features are phenomenally accessible in the *Vita Nuova*. In the *canzone* "Donne ch'avete," for example, Dante alludes to certain of his lady's features: her mouth, her eyes, and so forth. The body of Beatrice, on the other hand, is never phenomenally accessible in itself. *It is the temporal locus of animation that authenticates the transcendence of her phenomenality.*

Much of the burden of the subsequent investigation will be to unfold the full meaning of this abstract statement. Meanwhile we can remark that the phenomenality of Beatrice—that is, that which appears to perception—translates into her beauty. Beatrice's aesthetic epiphany becomes the representation of her withdrawing body in a guise adequate to perception, much like the crimson veil, which provided a guise for perception in Dante's dream. We could go so far as to say that the crimson veil becomes a master figure for Beatrice's beauty, representing as it does the primordial guise in which she appears to aesthetic perception. What is "wondrous" about this beauty is the fact that it acts as the register of a noumenal presence, a presence that expropriates but also "inspires" her lover with poetry. It is no accident, after all, that the expropriation of Dante's heart in the dream generates the first poem of the *libello*. Arising from the otherness of Beatrice's presence, the poems are testimonies to such events of expropriation, even after Beatrice has died.

For what does it mean, finally, that Beatrice "inspires" a poem? As we will see in the following chapter, it means that the poem incorporates the animations of her presence into its own new life, and that poetic language becomes in some sense authenticated or substantiated by virtue of its genesis. This lyric of incorporation, which opens up to its transcendent genesis, sets Dante apart from the two other major lyricists of the medieval Italian tradition, Cavalcanti and Petrarch. With both Cavalcanti and Petrarch the absence of any substantial access to otherness becomes a poetic ideology and condition in itself. In Cavalcanti's case the absence turns into a verbal space of noetic exile; in Petrarch's case, into the solipsistic sighs of lament. Each in his own way reveals the degree to which Dante's poetics is committed to a wholly different agenda that leads in the direction of comedy. By considering the case of Cavalcanti and Petrarch we will better be able to see that what motivates Dante's lyric and allows him eventually to transcend its confines is its mediated access to the body of Beatrice.

The *Vita Nuova* ends with a vow on Dante's part to remain silent until he may speak of Beatrice more worthily. The failure to speak of her adequately, to disclose the meaning of her presence on earth, to say of her what has not been said of any woman—these failures that bring the *Vita Nuova* to an unresolved close contain retroreferences to Dante's failure "to see" the true meaning of his "marvelous vision." In both cases the failures involve poetic genesis. In the case of the marvelous vision they initiate the literary enterprise that gets suspended at the end of the work, while the failures announced at the end mark a new breakthrough in Dante's understanding of his enterprise, an understanding that allows him to tell the story of his past and at the same time to envision a literary destiny for the future. What seems certain is that this projective literary career receives its initial stimulus in chapter III of the *Vita Nuova*, in a visionary moment of remote proximity to the body of Beatrice. Never again, not even in paradise, will Dante be so near to Beatrice. The intimate distance of a veil that holds him off from her naked presence gradually becomes the vast expanse of a cosmos that the poet will traverse in an inexorable venture of representation.

2 The Ideal Lyric

The *Vita Nuova* contains different kinds of poems: poems of bewilderment, of enchantment, of self-pity, of mourning; occasional poems; pedantic poems; and even unfinished poems. In this chapter, I privilege only one of these poems, the sonnet "Tanto gentile" in chapter XXVI. With this sonnet, the lyric ambition achieves its most sublime expression, giving rise to what I would call Dante's "ideal lyric." Before we turn to it, however, let us see why it deserves to be singled out with such a label.

When the protagonist of the *Divine Comedy* encounters Bonagiunta Orbicciani on the terrace of the gluttons in *Purgatorio* XXIV, that rhymester from Lucca recognizes the lyric poet of the *Vita Nuova*:

> "Ma dì s'i' veggio qui colui che fore
> trasse le nove rime, cominciando
> '*Donne ch'avete intelletto d'amore.*' "
> E io a lui: "I' mi son un che, quando
> Amor mi spira, noto, e a quel modo
> ch'e' ditta dentro vo significando."
> "O frate, issa veggi' io," diss' elli, "il nodo
> che 'l Notaro e Guittone e me ritenne
> di qua dal dolce stil novo ch'i' odo!
> Io veggio ben come le vostre penne
> di retro al dittator sen vanno strette,
> che le nostre certo non avvenne;
> e qual più a gradire oltre si mette,
> non vede più da l'uno a l'altro stilo";
> e, quasi contentato, si tacette.   (LL. 49–63)

"But tell me if the man whom I see here
is he who brought the new rhymes forth, beginning:
'*Ladies who have intelligence of love.*' "
I answered: "I am one who, when Love breathes
in me, takes note; what he, within, dictates,
I, in that way, without, would speak and shape."
"O brother, now I see," he said, "the knot
that kept the Notary, Guittone, and me
short of the sweet new manner that I hear.
I clearly see how your pens follow closely
behind him who dictates, and certainly
that did not happen with our pens; and he
who sets himself to ferreting profoundly
can find no other differences between
the two styles." He fell still, contentedly.

This frequently cited passage stands as Dante's posthumous comment on the poetics that underlies his ideal lyric. The pilgrim identifies himself to Bonagiunta in terms of a poetics of inspiration, and Bonagiunta reacts by pluralizing the protagonists on either side of the "sweet new manner" that he hears in Dante's words.[1] Thanks to this pluralization we now speak of the poetic "school" of the *Dolce stil novo,* or stilnovism. Scholars have debated the formal existence of such a school, but few will deny that around Tuscany toward the end of the thirteenth century there arose, whether formally or informally, a new generation of vernacular lyricists who magnified the spiritual vocation of the love passion and invested the poetic mission with a wholly new, intellectual dignity. This new generation included the younger Dante, Cavalcanti, Cino da Pistoia, Lapo Gianni, and others, with Guido Guinizelli as the group's authority figure.[2] However loosely one wants to group the individual practices of these poets, the "new" elements in stilnovism are its radical interiorization of the lyric subject and an implantation of esoteric knowledge into the domain of poetic theory and praxis. One could say that a preoccupation with epistemology and metaphysics, an uncompromised quest for the limits of figurative language, and an extravagant noetic claim for poetry distinguish the stilnovists from their Italian predecessors, predecessors like Jacopo da Lentini ("il Notaro"), Guittone d'Arezzo, and Bonagiunta himself, among others. These same features distinguish the stilnovists from the Provençal tradition of courtly poetry.[3]

A profound enigma lies at the heart of stilnovism, however, which has to do with the still-unclarified relation between inspiration and intellection. We know that the historical Bonagiunta once addressed a sonnet to the historical Guinizelli in which he accused the latter of having "changed the manner" of love poetry by exploiting a professorial erudition rather than the sincerity of sentiment, implicitly suggesting an opposition between poetic inspiration as it was traditionally understood and intellectual cognition and learning.[4] In *Purgatory*, however, Dante has Bonagiunta confess that while he was alive he was unable to see how the new intellectual love poetry actually sprang from a deeper source of inspiration: "I' mi son un che, quando / Amor mi spira, noto, e a quel modo / ch'è ditta dentro vo significando." Bonagiunta's recantation is expressed already in his citation of the inspired first verse of Dante's *canzone* "Donne ch'avete intelletto d'amore," a poem which seeks to establish a primordial link between love and intellection. What is this link all about, and how does it lead us back to the presence of Beatrice? We must look for answers in the genesis of the *canzone* cited by Bonagiunta.

In a well-known episode of the *Vita Nuova*, Dante describes his decision to seek his happiness nowhere else but "in those words that laud my lady" [*quelle parole che lodano la donna mia*]. Earlier in the narrative he had sought his happiness in Beatrice's salvific greeting, which she one day decided to deny him because of his objectionable comportment toward another woman.[5] Dante's new source of happiness—the epideictic lyric—will prove no more stable or permanent than the previous one, since Beatrice will die not long after the poet discovers praise as the vocation of his lyric; nonetheless, the poet's resolve to write only laudatory poetry marks one of the dramatic turning points not only of the *Vita Nuova* but of European literary history in general, for the epideictic convention later crytallized by Petrarchism dominates literary practices for some two or more centuries after Dante discovers praise as the only language adequate for Beatrice.[6] Dante, to be sure, does not invent the epideictic love lyric, but his discovery of it as a poetic vocation in the *Vita Nuova* remains an emblematic moment and, if nothing else, gives rise to the finest poems in the book, including the *canzone* "Donne ch'avete."

Praise is without doubt the inner, nostalgic vocation of poetry in general. Poetic praise allows that which is praised—the hero, the athlete, the statesman, the lady, the homeland, the mountains, the "lake effects," the seasons of nature—to reveal itself in its own essential light, which is not the light of poetry but which, without poetry, lacks the space in which to shine forth. Thus Kierkegaard, deploying a classical topos developed by Horace, can say that the hero needs the poet to become the hero that he already is by virtue of his deeds, and the poet in turn needs his hero to become the poet that he is.[7] Whatever poetry has not gathered up in its ontological celebration will ultimately have no lasting being, for, to speak with Friedrich Hölderlin, "that which endures is established by poets."[8] The onto-dependence that obtains between the praiser and the praised cannot in this sense simply be traced back to mechanisms of poetic subjectivity, with all that the concept of poetic subjectivity has come to imply in recent literary criticism. Can we think of a Pindarian ode in terms of a "subject" constituting itself by its objective praise of an Olympic victor? Rather, the athlete's excellence, or *arete*, comes forth in the epideictic poem as the defining light of perfection, or as the fulfilled onto-potential ("become who you already are") which marks the victor at the moment of his glory, when he stands out in the radiance of achievement. It is this radiance of achieved being that shines in the poet's praise irrevocably. Ontopoetry of this sort, which offers in praise the place where something may stand out in its own perfection, lies well beyond the troubled sphere of poetic "subjectivity."[9]

But epideictic poetry is not always ontopoetry in this sense. The love poem brings with it a specific kind of tension that engenders a full-fledged poetic subject, a subject born in the womb of reflexivity insofar as its praise is sustained by a desire that experiences itself as lack, want, negativity, or nonachievement—in short, as a subjectivity defined by reference to some other transcendent term. Such desire creates the space of a relation that sets the subject in motion toward its eventual coincidence with an object that would bring the relation to closure. The love poem is thus haunted, even if only rhetorically, by the immanence of finitude; the praiser becomes a subject of desire defined negatively in relation to the desired object of praise.

But in the final analysis the constitution of such subjectivity relies largely on the resources of rhetoric. The epideictic subject reappropriates itself—that is to say, constitutes its subjectivity—in the act of poetic praise itself, which means in the achieved poem and not in any presumed transcendence of the distance that holds subject and object apart in a specular relation to each other. How could Dante otherwise presume to find his happiness in "those words that laud my lady"? Love poetry thus becomes love of poetry, praise becomes an implicit celebration of the poem in which the woman is celebrated, or, as Joel Fineman puts it, "praise is an objective showing [deixis] that is essentially subjective showing off" on the part of the poet.[10]

The *Vita Nuova* both confirms and defies such notions of lyric subjectivity. The complications arise as soon as we confront the status of the other in the life of the poem, for the love poem's subject is defined or constituted by virtue of the mode in which it articulates its subjection to the other. Hence it becomes necessary to schematize the various essential modes of lyric subjection. Such a schematization would not allow us to speak of "Dante and Petrarch" in the same breath, for example, or of "Dante and Cavalcanti," without a series of qualifications. While these masters of the Italian lyric belong to the same larger epideictic tradition of love poetry, the ideologies that sustain their work are at such fundamental variance that, together, the poets form a trinity of differences which paradigmatically dominates the alternatives of the lyric enterprise. What distinguishes them in their trinitarian unity is precisely the status of the other in relation to which a poetic subjectivity is constituted (Petrarch), dissolved (Cavalcanti), or overcome (Dante). The importance of the *Vita Nuova* for this schematization lies in the self-consciousness with which it brings together in confrontation the opposed ideologies that underlie these paradigmatic alternatives. The story of Dante's disorientations, his false starts and breakthroughs, his continuous gropings for the poetic voice and an authentic idiom, makes the early work a space of encounter for the various poetic options that the poet adopts, abandons, transforms, or discovers. The story of these options is the implicit and still untold story of the *libello*.

Dante's decision to seek his happiness only in those words that praise his lady marks the most consequential moment in that story, so consequential that Dante will invoke it in *Purgatorio* xxiv to define the poetics that presumably guides him toward the recovery of Beatrice in the earthly paradise.[11] In the *Vita Nuova*, Dante very subtly describes a brief period of suspension between his resolution to embrace the epideictic style and the first poem in that "new manner." It is not merely a moment of hesitation; above all, it is a moment of reflection. This motif of reflection becomes central in chapter xix, where Dante recounts the genesis of the *canzone* "Donne ch'avete" in terms of both inspiration and reflection:

> Avvenne poi che passando per uno cammino lungo lo quale sen gia uno rivo chiaro molto, a me giunse tanta volontade di dire, che io cominciai a pensare lo modo ch'io tenesse; e pensai che parlare di lei non si convenia che io facesse, se io non parlasse a donne in se-

conda persona, e non ad ogni donna, ma solamente a coloro che sono gentili e che non sono pure femmine. Allora dico che la mia lingua parlò quasi come per se stessa mossa, e disse: *Donne ch'avete intelletto d'amore.* Queste parole io ripuosi ne la mente con grande letizia, pensando di prenderle per mio cominciamento; onde poi, ritornato a la sopradetta cittade, pensando alquanti die, cominciai una canzone con questo cominciamento, ordinata nel modo che si vedrà di sotto ne la sua divisione. La canzone comincia: *Donne ch'avete.* (XIX, 1-4)

It then happened that, while I was walking on a path along which ran a clear river, I was seized by a desire to speak, and I began to think of the manner I had resolved upon, and I thought that I should not address [Beatrice] except by addressing women in the second person, and not all women but only those who are gentle. I say that then my tongue spoke almost as if it were moved of its own accord, and it said: *Ladies Who Have Intelligence of Love.* I put these words away in my mind with great joy, thinking to take them as my beginning; and so, once I had returned to the above mentioned town, I began a *canzone* with this beginning, ordered in the manner which will be seen in the division below. The *canzone* begins: "Ladies Who Have."

Punctuated with the word *cominciamento*, the passage can be taken to describe the genesis not only of a poem but also of stilnovism as an ideal synthesis of inspiration and intellection. The first verse of the *canzone* seems to come to Dante as naturally as the flow of the clear river along which he is walking (the river as an analogy for the inspired flow of poetic speech will be exploited later by Petrarch in the famous "Chiare, fresche e dolci acque," which I discuss in chapter 5). But we notice that the poet immediately consigns that first verse to his mind, submitting its inspiration to reflection (*pensando alquanti die*) before composing the poem according to a rigorous and elaborate structure. We also notice that even before the verse comes to him, it seems as if the poet's reflection *induces* the form that inspiration will take: he is seized by the desire to speak, then he thinks about the manner (*pensare lo modo*), then he thinks (*pensai*) that he should address women in the second person, and so on.[12] What begins here is not simply an inspired *canzone* later cited by Bonagiunta in *Purgatory*, but a new manner of poetic composition in which the supreme theme of praise is able, so it seems, to bring about a fusion of inspiration and intellection. The poem generated on this occasion of ideal synthesis marks Dante's first breakthrough into the hyperspace of poetic praise.[13] Toward the end of this chapter we will see that this synthesis is not the full story, and that a stubborn tension keeps inspiration and intellection at odds.

Since "Donne ch'avete" is not the ideal lyric that most concerns me in this chapter, I shall not presume to analyze it in any depth. What interests me above all in the *canzone* is the way in which poetic praise takes the form of a Thomistic aestheticization of the figure of Beatrice. Why do praise, inspiration, and intellection come together in an aesthetics of beauty? Why is beauty the inevitable synthetic phenomenon that sustains Dante's "new manner"? I shall attempt to answer the questions one step at a time, beginning with an example of how the new style entails an aesthetic transfiguration of Beatrice. The fourth stanza of "Donne ch'avete" may serve as our example:

> Dice di lei Amor: "Cosa mortale
> come esser pò sì adorna e sì pura?"
> Poi la reguarda, e fra se stesso giura
> che Dio ne 'ntenda di far cosa nova.
> Color di perle ha quasi, in forma quale
> convene a donna aver, non for misura:
> ella è quanto de ben pò far natura;

per essemplo di lei bieltà si prova.
De li occhi suoi, come ch'ella li mova,
escono spiriti d'amore inflammati,
che feron li occhi a qual che allor la guati,
e passan sì che 'l cor ciascun retrova:
voi le vedete Amor pinto nel viso,
la 've non pote alcun mirarla fiso.

(LL. 44–56)

> Love says of her: "How can a mortal thing
> be so adorned and yet so pure?"
> Then he looks at her and swears within himself
> that God intended to make something new.
> She is almost the color of pearl, in the form
> appropriate to a woman, not out of proportion:
> she is the best that nature can produce;
> she is the very exemplum of beauty.
> As she moves her eyes, inflamed spirits
> of love leave them and strike one's eyes,
> and find the heart of everyone [who looks at her]:
> you see love painted on her face,
> there where no one can look fixedly at her.

The epideictic manner phenomenalizes Beatrice to a truly hyperbolic extreme. Throughout the poem she appears to satisfy the three conditions for beauty elaborated by Thomas Aquinas: *integritas, consonantia,* and *claritas.*[14] There are important reasons for invoking Thomas Aquinas in this context; not only does the Scholastic language of potency and act pervade Dante's *divisioni* once the poems of praise are in question (xix–xxi), but the laudatory thrust of the *canzone* entails a wholly Thomistic aesthetic reification of Beatrice, who is spoken of as a "cosa nova" imbued with luminosity. The angels clamor to God in the second stanza about a soul on earth whose *active* light reaches the summits of heaven. Why is Beatrice praised in terms of radiance, and how does this bring us into the sphere of a Thomistic aesthetics?

Thomas Aquinas conceived of beauty in terms of a paradoxical relation between adequation and transcendence. *Pulchritudo* belongs among the transcendentals (*ens, res, unum, aliquid, bonum,* and *verum*), but what makes it unique is that the beautiful "thing" unites these transcendentals within itself and allows them to shine forth phenomenally.[15] Aquinas's word for this radiance is *claritas.* More precisely, *claritas* means the radiance of form permeating a thing and adequating it to intellectual apprehension on a human scale.[16] Coming ultimately from God, it illuminates the material opacity of a thing so that, through the agency of sense perception, the intellect may identify the thing by its form. The importance of the aesthetic category comes from the human intellect's inability to apprehend something apart from the agency of the senses.[17] But because we perceive through them, the senses for Aquinas are a cognitive agency, unlike, for example, the will. We know through sensation. In this respect we may say that for Aquinas beauty is always embodied and is always form's inhabitation of a material density; thus, it occurs essentially in *entities.*

In "Donne ch'avete" Dante insists upon not only Beatrice as an entity imbued with luminosity, but Beatrice *as an entity.* In her case, beauty occurs in a "cosa nova," a new thing—new to the extent that she is pure (i.e., luminous) and at the same time adorned or veiled (i.e., opaque). Thus, in verses 43-44 of the *canzone* we confront a question that sums up the true enigma of Beatrice's beauty: "Dice di lei Amor: 'Cosa mortale / come esser pò sì adorna e sì pura?'" ["Love says of her: 'How can a mortal thing be so adorned and yet so pure?' "]. The question asks about the aesthetic coincidence between the phenomenal and noumenal dimensions of Beatrice, dimensions that I tried to conceive of as a differentiated unity in my earlier discussion of the body and its veil.

Now, it is essential to aesthetic theories that they articulate the difference between a beautiful *thing* on the one hand and the aesthetic *emotion* it brings about on the other. The latter is more elusive and opaque, harder to define, precisely because it

has more to do with appetition than intellection. The move is
from aesthetic object to aesthetic subject. On another plane,
the move is also one from intellection to inspiration.[18] It is one
thing to describe the aesthetic exemplarity or "thinghood" of
Beatrice, as Dante does in "Donne ch'avete," but it is quite another to describe the inner motions of the aesthetic emotion as
such, which is what Dante does in the "Tanto gentile" sonnet. I
give "Tanto gentile" the label of Dante's ideal lyric simply because it embodies the primordial emotion of poetic inspiration
described by Dante in *Purgatorio* xxiv. But to appreciate fully
the achievement of the sonnet, let us first turn once more to
Thomas Aquinas, the essence of whose theory about the aesthetic emotion is remarkably embodied in Dante's poem.

Pulchra dicuntur quae visa placent: "We call beautiful those
things which, when seen, please."[19] With this definition
Aquinas sums up his insight into aesthetic emotion, leaving
us to wonder at its apparent simplicity. The definition is less
simple than it appears. To begin with, we must in no way think
of aesthetic "pleasure" as its core. To please here means not so
much to gratify but rather "to placate." Placation, and not pleasure, is the essence of the experience of the beautiful. This is
confirmed by Aquinas's comments on the effects of the beautiful on an observer, for instance: "Ad rationem pulchri pertinet
quod in eius aspectu seu cognitione *quietetur* appetitus" ["but it
pertains to the nature of the beautiful that, in knowing it, the
appetite finds rest"].[20] What the beautiful brings to repose, or
quiets and placates, is the restless commotion of appetition. It is
as if the aesthetic subject is released from the promotions of his
or her interested will, or from the commotions of subjectivity
itself. The appetite is not merely satisfied but placated. This
happens through the faculty of sight, which for Aquinas is a
faculty of knowledge. The beautiful differs from the good and
the true precisely because contemplation is induced through
the faculty of sight.[21]

We can enhance the insight into Aquinas's conception of
the beautiful by invoking a text that would seem to lie well out-

side the present context. There is a passage in James Joyce's *Portrait of the Artist as a Young Man* where Stephen Dedalus is discussing Aquinas's aesthetic theory with a friend. Stephen offers the following condensed but accurate account of it: "The instant," says Stephen, "wherein that supreme quality of beauty, the clear radiance of the esthetic image, is apprehended luminously by the mind which has been arrested by its wholeness and fascinated by its harmony is the luminous silent stasis of esthetic pleasure."[22] Stephen works the three conditions for the beautiful—*claritas, integritas* and *consonantia*—into his account, but what is uncannily insightful is his emphasis on the *instant* of arrestation, of placation, and his characterization of this instant as the "luminous silent stasis" of aesthetic experience. Although the instant is discrete and spontaneous, it nevertheless involves a process. It is this process of arrestation and aesthetic placation that Dante's ideal lyric embodies in its incorporation of Beatrice's presence:

> Tanto gentile e tanto onesta pare
> la donna mia quand'ella altrui saluta,
> ch'ogne lingua deven tremando muta,
> e li occhi no l'ardiscon di guardare.
>
> Ella si va, sentendosi laudare,
> benignamente d'umiltà vestuta;
> e par che sia una cosa venuta
> da cielo in terra a miracol mostrare.
>
> Mostrasi sì piacente a chi la mira,
> che dà per li occhi una dolcezza al core
> che'ntender no la può chi no la prova:
>
> e par che da la sua labbia si mova
> un spirito soave pien d'amore,
> che va dicendo a l'anima: Sospira.
> (xxvi, 5–8)

> So gentle and so honest appears
> my lady when she greets others,

that every tongue, trembling, becomes mute,
and eyes do not dare look on her.

She passes by, hearing herself praised,
benignly dressed in humility;
and she seems a thing come
from heaven to earth to show a miracle.

She appears so pleasing to who looks at her
that through the eyes she sends a sweetness to the heart
that cannot be known by who never has felt it:

and it seems that from her face moves
a soft spirit full of love
that goes straight to the soul saying: Sigh.

Beatrice has become a phenomenon of pure manifestation. Her epiphany silences the tongue and captivates the eye. The world comes to a rapturous halt as she passes by and dissolves the beholder's subjectivity in a sigh. The second verse, alluding to her greeting, already announces the expropriation of the poetic subject: "quand'ella altrui saluta." The word *altrui* contains a benign irony, for while Beatrice greets others, we know that she denies to Dante this same greeting. But the willful abstention of Dante's desire, or the release from its subjectivity, is the very precondition for Beatrice's appearance in her unconditional autonomy, heightened by the reflexive pronoun in formulations like "ella *si* va," "sentendo*si*," and "Mostra*si*."

"This sonnet is so easy to understand," says Dante in the prose of chapter XXVI, "that it needs no division." If its meaning is so manifest as to allow Dante to dispense with the customary exercise of dividing his poems, it is because the meaning of Beatrice comes forth in appearance. The miracle of her presence resides in its translation into a phenomenon of beauty. Beatrice shows. The *capfinidas* "mostrare" in verses 8–9 leave no doubt about the ostention of her being in the world: "una cosa venuta / da ceilo in terra a miracol *mostrare.* / *Mostrasi* sì piacente a chi la mira." She has become, in other words, an aesthetic event.

The entire lyric project of the *Vita Nuova* lies in the sigh that ends the poem and brings its subject to rest in aesthetic stasis. Here Beatrice no longer incites desire but placates it. This final sigh seems like a resignation to her intangible otherness but also figures as the inspiration that she dispenses through her proximity. The motion and rhythm of the verses seem to reproduce a deep intake and expiration of animating breath.[23] While the poem consummates itself in the sigh, the final expiration also marks the beginning of a lyric retrieval of the plenitude of presence. It consummates the lyric enunciation at the very moment that it initiates the recovery of aesthetic grace, for the poem issues forth from the sigh in which it culminates. The sigh forms, therefore, what one could call a lyric circle of incorporation. The voice cannot speak in Beatrice's presence ("ogne lingua deven tremando muta"), yet the sigh receives the breath of life given by the proximity of Beatrice. Thus animated, the lyric voice may speak the words "tanto gentile e tanto onesta pare / la donna mia," that is to say, its speech has been given life. The body of Beatrice moves as the locus of her presence animates the lyric which incorporates that presence into its speech, such that the rhythm of Beatrice's gait before the eyes of her beholders sustains the rhythm of the verses that move toward the final sigh.

Aesthetic stasis, then, is not an absence of motion; on the contrary, it is what Stephen Dedalus, in the same context from which I have quoted, calls the *rhythm* of beauty: "Beauty . . . cannot awaken in us an emotion which is kinetic or a sensation which is purely physical. It awakens, or ought to awaken, or induces, or ought to induce, an esthetic stasis, an ideal pity or an ideal terror, a stasis called forth, prolonged and at last dissolved by what I call the rhythm of beauty."[24] This rhythm that brings a turbulent subjectivity to repose belongs primordially to Beatrice and figures, in Dante's poem, as the pace of her passage through an array of spectators. While Beatrice arrests the spectators with her beauty, she herself passes. Placation takes place in the very rhythm with which her presence comes and goes. So while the final sigh culminates the experience of placation, it also gives vent to an absence in the soul as the passing of Beatrice deprives the poet of her propinquity.

The passage of Beatrice which arrests the world but which itself cannot be arrested—the gratuitous advent of her person that gives itself in beauty and yet holds itself back in the event of her presence—harbors the enigma of her withdrawing body. Here too in "Tanto gentile" the proximity of that body retreats behind a veil, a cloth, a dress of humility: "Ella si va, sentendosi laudare, / benignamente *d'umiltà vestuta.*" In the sonnet that follows, "Vede perfettamente onne salute," Beatrice is dressed in the virtues of gentleness, love, and faith ("vestuta / di gentilezza, d'amore, e di fede"). The dressed status of Beatrice is neither insignificant nor casual, for her noumenal body animates her phenomenal beauty, and this beauty, in turn, animates the poem whose breath expires in an incorporation of her presence. Praise of Beatrice thus becomes an index of the life she gives to the lyric.

How do things stand, then, between intellection and inspiration, the fusion of which seems to be the ideal of Dante's new laudatory lyric? In *Purgatory*, Bonagiunta cites the first verse of "Donne ch'avete." Dante responds by alluding to a poetics of inspiration. We have looked at the passage that describes the genesis of the *canzone* and have seen that the poem springs from a series of reflective interventions on Dante's part. It is willful, intellectualistic, and highly structured; even the first verse, which ostensibly was the result of an inspiration, came to the poet only after he had deliberated and "thought" about the manner in which he would compose a poem ("Io cominciai a *pensare* lo modo . . . e *pensai* che parlare di lei," etc.). More importantly, the poem originates in reflective solitude, while Dante walks along a riverbank. It does *not* originate in the presence of Beatrice, as the "Tanto gentile" sonnet does. These two poems essentially refer to radically different orders of poetic experience, even though they seem to belong to the same generic laudatory style. The "inspired" poem is, in a quite literal sense,

"Tanto gentile." The sigh that forms its lyric circle of incorporation and that comes from Beatrice's proximity is fundamentally different from the reflective and solitary "inspiration" of the rationalistic *canzone*. The ideal lyric is in some sense beyond intellection.

It is not accidental that Dante divides and subdivides "Donne ch'avete" more scrupulously than any other poem in the *Vita Nuova* and that he dispenses with the exercise altogether in the case of "Tanto gentile." As we will see in the following chapter, Dante's *divisioni* are supposed to lay bare the *intelligible* structure of the poems, or their so-called *ragione*. But for some reason the *ragione* of the inspired poem cannot be "denuded" in the same way as the poem of intellection. The reason for this takes us to the heart of the *Vita Nuova*—the heart that still inhabits the body of Beatrice.

3 Figures of Love

Hypostasis   Through veils of beauty that provoke
wonder about her provenance, the
body of Beatrice gives itself to the world as an epiphanic, public
event. Her presence, dispensing grace and gratitude among her
spectators, comes as a gift at once given and giving. The ideal
lyric flourishes in her radiant sphere, but like a great solar mass
benign from a distance, her presence can become overbearing if
the poet strays too close to her. The *Vita Nuova* describes such
moments of overbearing proximity. In xiv we find Dante being
led by a friend to a wedding festival in a Florentine house, "so
that [the ladies present] might be served [by Dante and his
friend] in a worthy manner" (xiv, 3). Dante does not suspect
that Beatrice is among the women gathered there, and, standing in the room unawares, he feels a tremor in the left side of his
body:

> E nel fine del mio proponimento mi parve sentire uno
> mirabile tremore incominciare nel mio petto da la sini-
> stra parte e distendersi di subito per tutte le parti del
> mio corpo. Allora dico che io poggiai la mia persona
> simultamente ad una pintura la quale circundava
> questa mangione; e temendo non altri si fosse accorto
> del mio tremare, levai li occhi, e mirando le donne,
> vidi tra loro la gentilissima Beatrice. (xiv, 4–5)

> And after reaching my decision I seemed to feel a mi-
> raculous tremor begin in the left side of my chest and
> spread immediately throughout all the parts of my

47

> body. I say, then, that I pretended to lean my body
> against the painted walls of this house; and fearing
> that others had become aware of my trembling, I
> raised my eyes and, gazing at the women, I saw among
> them the most gentle Beatrice.

The scene epitomizes what I have tried to stress about Beatrice: that her *presence* and her *appearance* must be thought of as a unity, yet differentiated. Before Beatrice is perceived with the eyes, her presence already induces physiological disorder in her lover. As the locus of presence, her body precedes and at the same time withdraws behind her phenomenality, such that presence and appearance form a unity and not a compound. The discrete nature of this unity has caused critics to overlook its differentiated character and to emphasize the figurative, analogical, or referential terms in which Beatrice appears throughout the *Vita Nuova*: as Christ figure, as angel, as number nine, as phantasm, as beatifier, as Ciceronian "friend," etc. It is this "as factor" that guards and conceals the body of Beatrice. It indicates that she is accessible only in this or that phenomenal mode, and that her "meaning" is given through a series of figurative veils. But by emphasizing the set of terms that follow the "as factor," scholars allow the genetic principle that makes Beatrice the locus of so many figurative accretions to slip into oblivion. Expressed otherwise, the body that retreats behind her modes of access remains literally "overlooked."

We must be careful not to pursue any one of the various analogical or figurative determinations of Beatrice too far, for to do so leads to insurmountable contradictions. For example, much has been made of the fact that Beatrice is associated with the number nine in the *Vita Nuova*, but no one, to my knowledge, has interrogated Dante's logic in xxix when he explains that this number was linked to Beatrice because nine is a "divine" number: the Trinity times itself. Is Dante telling his reader that Beatrice is or was a Trinity figure? If so, can she also logically be a Christ figure? And if she is a Christ figure, can she also logically be an angel figure? And can she, in addition to these determinations, also be a historical woman? The *Vita Nuova* will elude us on this score unless we take a step back to the "as factor" and interrogate the hypostasis of Beatrice which allows for such a proliferation of analogical determinations associated with her person.[1]

The hypostasis of Beatrice centers around the manner in which she substantializes love. In *Purgatorio* xxiv, where Dante revisits his lyric past, he declares: " I' mi son un che, quando / Amor mi spira, noto, e a quel modo / ch'e' ditta dentro vo significando." We have discussed the differences between "Donne ch'avete" and the ideal lyric, "Tanto gentile." In one case a poem is inspired autonomously and intellectually; in the other it is Beatrice herself who inspires a sigh of aesthetic stasis. Theoretically speaking, the stilnovist could claim that in both cases love, or *Amor*, is the agent of inspiration. One of the "new" aspects of stilnovism was the hypostasis of love as an abstract and ideal universal. The question of the nature or essence of love is the overriding question not only of Dante's *libello* but of stilnovism in general. Guinizelli's "Al cor gentile," Cavalcanti's "Donna me prega," and Dante's *Vita Nuova*, all represent answers to that one question which had become a veritable theoretical obsession among the poets of this school: What is love? When Dante composed "Donne ch'avete" he was firmly committed to the hypostasis of love as an independent and autonomous agent. This is evident from the poem that follows "Donne ch'avete" in chapter xx. Asked by a friend to "say what love is," Dante composed a sonnet in which love appears as a hypostasized and abstract entity:

> Amore e 'l cor gentil sono una cosa,
> sì come il saggio in suo dittare pone,
> e così esser l'un sanza l'altro osa
> com'alma razional sanza ragione.
>
> Falli natura quand'è amorosa,
> Amor per sire e 'l cor per sua magione,

dentro la qual dormendo si riposa
tal volta poca e tal lunga stagione.

Bieltate appare in saggia donna pui,
che piace a gli occhi sì, che dentro al core
nasce un disio de la cosa piacente;

e tanto dura talora in costui,
che fa svegliare lo spirito d'Amore.
E simil face in donna omo valente.

(xx, 3–6)

Love and the gentle heart are one thing,
as the sage [Guinizelli] declares in his poem,
and one cannot be without the other
any more than the rational soul can be without reason.

Nature makes them when she is in love,
love as lord and the heart as its dwelling place,
in which love can rest as he sleeps,
at times for a short while, at times for longer.

Then beauty appears in a virtuous woman,
pleasing the eyes so much that, within the heart,
a desire for the delightful thing is born;

and it dwells there [in the heart]
until the spirit of love is woken.
And a worthy man does the same in a woman.

The sonnet is something of a vulgarization of Guinizelli's "Al cor gentile," which, as we remarked, had become for the stilnovists a declaration of faith. The banality of the poem's citational gesture and its retreat into the protective shadow of an authority figure represent a dramatic fall from the creative experiment of "Donne ch'avete," yet in some ways the sonnet merely formalizes, doctrinally, the vision of love which is operative in the preceding *canzone*.[2] Six chapters later, however, a reversal has clearly taken place: the hypostasis of love gives way to the hypostasis of Beatrice. The ideal lyric is born directly as a result of this reversal. Let us see how it takes place.

Chapter xxiv, which marks one of the turning points in the *Vita Nuova*, describes a remarkable scene: Dante is sitting in some public place and his heart begins to tremble as if he was in the presence of his lady. The lord of love appears in his imagination—the same lord who appeared to Dante in the "marvelous vision" and who has since held sway over him. This time, however, the lord is full of joy. He tells Dante to consider himself blessed. Dante then sees a beautiful woman, not in his imagination but in the public place where he is sitting, whom he recognizes as the lady loved by his friend Guido. She is Giovanna. Following close behind her is the marvelous Beatrice. The lord announces to Dante that he had inspired Guido to give Giovanna the *senhal* "Primavera" for this occasion alone, when she would *come before* Beatrice ("prima verrà"). Even her proper name, Giovanna, derives its true significance from St. John the Baptist ("Giovanni"), who preceded the true light of Christ, the way Giovanna precedes Beatrice on this triumphant day in the streets of Florence. So speaks the lord. With the lord's final words this enigmatic figure of speech transfers his essence over to the supreme figure of Beatrice: "E chi volesse sottilmente considerare, quella Beatrice chiamerebbe Amore, per molta simiglianza che ha meco" (xxiv, 5) ["And whoever thinks subtly about Beatrice would call her love, because of the great similitude that she bears to me"].

With these words the lord dissolves his status as a personification and disappears from the narrative once and for all. In xxv Dante exposes him as nothing more than a figure of speech. The reason is quite simple: Beatrice has become, at this point in the narrative, the proper name of love. Her person has substantialized the accident, so to speak. It is in these terms that we must understand the Christological references in xxiv: as an authentication of Beatrice's singular and substantial embodiment of love itself. The person of Beatrice has turned the lord into a superfluous and ultimately illegitimate personification.[3]

Let us reflect on the question, for it involves not only the essence of love but also love's topology. One of the peculiar characteristics of the *Vita Nuova* is the impression it creates of having originated from out of itself by virtue of its own autonomous visionary energy. The narrative insists on bracketing anything like a real world outside the poet's imagination in order to blur the boundaries between a public street and a private hallucination, between an actual event like Beatrice's death and a delirious dream that foreshadows it. Opacity, ambiguity, paronomasia, and allusion are some of the techniques whereby the book seeks to represent not the facts of experience but the transformation they undergo in the phantasmal interiority of the poet's "memoria." As Cavalcanti had declared in "Donna me prega," love has its true place not in the external world but in this imaginary space of memory. But the fact is that the *Vita Nuova* moves both inward and outward, from figure to body, from substance to image, from bedroom to street, and vice versa.[4] The demise of the lord in xxiv in fact marks a decisive turn in the very experience of love, a turn toward exteriority and otherness that commits Dante to the irreducibility of the embodied historical world itself. During that episode the lord appears to Dante in his imagination, that is to say, in the psychic space of inner vision. But it is precisely there that Dante is enjoined by the lord to look outward to the transcendent Beatrice. The world—that is where love has its proper place. Transcendence, in other words, is externalized and embodied. Love traverses the boundaries of psychic interiority and enters the arena of existential facticity.

I am not suggesting that Dante merely shifts the locus of love away from the imagination to substantial "reality," whatever that may be, but that the inner impulse of his enterprise is to link the phantasmal with historicity, opening the horizons of both to an essential interaction. Beatrice is without question caught up in the logic of the image, but her corporeality is immediate and irreducible to a mere phantasmology. It is important to stress the point, for it is here that an acute critic of medieval love poetry like Giorgio Agamben seems to overlook the differential element in Dante's early poetics with regard to the work of other stilnovists. Agamben writes:

> The medieval discovery of love by the Provençal and stilnovist poets is . . . the discovery that love has as its direct object not the sensible thing [*la cosa sensibile*] but the phantasm; that is to say, it is simply the discovery of the phantasmic character of love. . . . Insofar as love has its proper place in the imagination [*fantasia*], desire never finds before itself the object in its corporeality (hence the apparent "Platonism" of troubadoric/ stilnovistic eros) but rather [finds before itself] an image.[5]

The statement is remarkable both for its concision and for its insight, yet even the most penetrating generic statements about stilnovism run into trouble when the texts become specific. There is no doubt that the *Vita Nuova* brings the phantasmal dimension of love to a certain extreme with its visions, aesthetic epiphanies, and even hallucinations. On the other hand, if we put the troubadours, the stilnovists, Cavalcanti, and Dante within a single experiential horizon, we are bound to gloss over the way Dante redefines the troubadour and even the Cavalcantian notions of love. Beatrice is both body and image. Dante *does* find himself before her corporeal otherness, and it is precisely that otherness which remains in excess of the phantasm. The body of Beatrice assures her exteriority and literal historicity, just as it assures that she cannot be wholly reified.[6]

The body of Beatrice is that which psychic experience cannot assimilate or appropriate; it is the unreifiable dimension of her otherness which keeps Dante moving to and fro from private interiors (the "solingo luogo" of his bedroom) to the public spheres of Beatrice's epiphanies. For this reason the *Vita Nuova* cannot exclude the topology of the public sphere from the experience of love, the way the poems of Cavalcanti do. The private and public arenas of love become inseparable. The episode of

Dante's swooning in chapter XIV occurs in the only sphere where Beatrice can overwhelm her lover in the interiority of his being, namely, in a public sphere. Likewise, the ideal lyric "Tanto gentile" describes Beatrice's epiphany as a public event that engages the community at large. In a similar vein Dante will later speak of Florence as the "widowed city," deprived of her *beatrice*, or beatifier. If Dante resists the closure of Cavalcanti's interiorities; if he places his poems within the framework of an autobiographical narrative, and if much later he embraces the epic alternative, becoming the so-called poet of history, it is because he never ceased to acknowledge the exteriority of Beatrice or the historical otherness of her being in the world. It is this otherness that I have been calling her body.

Ironies of Literary Theory We must now confront one of the enigmas of the *Vita Nuova*. This is the digression into literary theory in chapter XXV. If in XXIV Dante dramatizes Beatrice's substantial embodiment of love in her person, then why does he open XXV with a reminder that love is not a substance but an accident occurring in a substance? Chapter XXV is one of the moments when the "veil" of the story is torn and the theoretical preoccupations underlying the *Vita Nuova* are revealed, lending credence to Edoardo Sanguineti's claim that the narrative dimension of the work is merely a cosmetics for what amounts to Dante's theoretical statement about poetics: "The novelistic form is a mere veil, continuously violated and torn, for an essayistic content, or theoretical discourse; because in essence the *Vita Nuova* is not a sustained narrative but rather a historical discourse [*ragionamento storico*] around an idea of poetry."[7] As I proceed in this section to highlight the literary theory in Dante's text, I shall also discuss the debates in literary theory which are taking place in our own day. We will see that Dante's theoretical preoccupations about the status of figurative language prefigure in a striking way the "tropological" reading of lyric poetry initiated by Paul de Man and taken up by other literary critics in what amounts to a major revision of our traditional conceptions of the lyric poem. But first let us examine Dante's reflections in xxv.

Chapter xxv presents itself as a digression in the narrative. Its ostensible purpose is to clear up misunderstandings the reader might have about the author's deployment of figurative language, and in particular about his personification of love as a "lord." Until the digression, Dante has personified love so consistently as to create the illusion of a veritable character in the story with an autonomous reality and will of his own. Chapter xxv wants to show that the author is in control of his use of figurative language, that is to say, that he controls the boundary line between figurative and literal signification. Thus he tells us that he has been speaking of love as if it were a corporeal substance ("si come fosse sustanzia corporale"), but that technically speaking love is merely an accident occurring in a substance. According to this definition (which Dante borrowed from his friend Cavalcanti), love has no substantiality or embodiment in itself and remains transcendent with regard to the corporeal substances in which it occurs (the accident literally "befalls" substance: *accidens*). Literally, therefore, love has no body or voice. If love takes on a body and voice and becomes anthropomorphic, it is only by virtue of poetic prosopopoeia. It is here, then, that Dante raises the question of the legitimacy of figurative speech: When may it be deployed, under what conditions is it valid, and who are the poets who rightfully have license to it? Dante's concern in xxv is to legitimate not only his personification of love—a personification he will in fact no longer employ—but also the poetic deployment of tropes in general.

The legitimation begins in an unusual manner, with an apology for composing in the vernacular. Here Dante proposes a theory for how vernacular poetry came into being: its origin is to be sought, so he claims, in the first poet's desire to convey his amorous sentiments to his lady, who knew little or no Latin. The desire for communciation, or the communciation of desire,

therefore, gives rise to the first attempts to rhyme in the vernacular. Since poets writing in Latin traditionally had poetic license to use various tropes and figures of speech, including the
personification of inanimate things, the vernacular versifier
may also enjoy such license.[8] But not indiscriminately. The license is granted only on the condition that the versifier be able
to divest his poem of its figurative components and expose the
poem's rational content in prose:

> Dunque, se noi vedemo che li poete hanno parlato a le
> cose inanimate, sì come se avessero senso e ragione, e
> fattele parlare insieme . . . degno è lo dicitore per rima
> di fare lo somigliante, ma non sanza ragione alcuna,
> ma con ragione la quale poi sia possibile d'aprire per
> prosa. (xxv, 8)

> Therefore, if these poets spoke to inanimate things as if
> they had sense and reason, and also gave them voice
> . . . the vernacular poet may do the same, but not
> without reason; rather with reasons that he can there-
> after expose in prose.

The issue of animation and the poetic voice becomes an
explicit theoretical problem here. Prosopopoeia and figures of
speech in general are justified in vernacular poetry only if they
contain *ragione*, or reason, or what Dante alternately calls
verace intendimento ("in guisa che [le parole] avessero verace intendimento," he says in the same passage).[9] Here we encounter
again the stilnovistic preoccupation with the role of intellection
in poetic composition. It is important to follow Dante's proposi-
tion here: the "true meaning" of the poet's words does not refer
to the literal content of figurative speech; it refers instead to the
logic that governs the conversion of literal into figurative signification or, better, to the principle of analogy and separation
which oversees the interplay between the two and polices the
boundary line between the literal and figurative. A worthy versifier is one who can expose, in prose, the principle of sufficient

reason underlying the external rhetoric of his poem, and he does this by decomposing its figures and laying bare the *ragione* that governs their deployment. Dante engages in precisely this sort of decomposition when he exposes the figure of prosopopoeia that allows him to speak of love as if it were an animate substance.[10]

We can already see that Dante is apologizing not only for the vernacular use of tropes but also for the *Vita Nuova* itself, which places poems side by side with a prose that presumably "opens up" the legitimating *ragione* that lies behind the poem's figurative components. We can also see that under the guise of ennobling vernacular poetry, he wants to erect standards, rules, and criteria by which the "worthy" vernacular poets may be distinguished from their unworthy counterparts. The challenge for Dante is to lay down standards that could establish an elitist poetics in the otherwise arbitrary sphere of the vernacular. One of the ironies of xxv, with its initial emphasis on the vernacular poet's desire to communicate to his lady, is that its discourse is motivated by Dante's desire for another kind of communication: not with his lady, who is already dead, but with his "primo amico" Guido Cavalcanti, to whom the *Vita Nuova* is dedicated.[11] As we learn in xxx, Guido was the one who encouraged Dante to write in the vernacular. So if vernacular poetry originally aimed to dissolve the exclusivity of poetry as an affair among poets only, the literary digression of xxv aims to reestablish precisely such exclusivity by positing criteria that separate the good poets from the bad (the stilnovist from the others), criteria that allow Dante to place himself alongside his illustrious friend Guido:

> dico che né li poete parlavano così sanza ragione, né quelli che rimano deono parlar così non avendo alcuno ragionamento in loro di quello che dicono; però che grande vergogna sarebbe a colui che rimasse cose sotto vesta di figura o di colore rettorico, e poscia, domandato, non sapesse denudare le sue parole da

cotale vesta, in guisa che avessero verace intendimento. E questo mio primo amico e io ne sapemo bene
di quelli che così rimano stoltamente. (xxv, 10)

I say that the poets did not speak so without reason,
nor should those who [now] rhyme speak without
reason in what they say; for it would be a great shame
if he who rhymed things under the dress of figures or
rhetorical colors could not, if asked, denude his words
of such a dress, to show that they contained true
meaning. And this best friend of mine and I know
plenty of such [poets] who compose in this crooked
fashion.

Dante's argument here is rich with ideological as well as
academic prejudices, with gestures of legislation, self-promo-
tion, and indeed, of self-misrepresentation. But let us bracket
the issue of legitimation for a moment and focus on the terms
Dante invokes to speak about figurative language, for they will
reveal the problematic nature of the entire chapter. They are
metaphorical terms familiar to us from another context: the
body and its dress. The former refers metaphorically to the
poem's *intendimento* and the latter to its poetic elements, especially its tropes and "rhetorical colors." Furthermore, Dante
calls for a prosaic "denudation" of the poetic dress (*vesta di figura*), a denudation that would lay bare its body, that is to say,
its *verace intendimento*. The oblique link between these metaphorical terms and the "marvelous vision" in chapter iii is far
from casual, although it is most certainly uncontrolled. Of crucial importance is the recurring correlation, in a wholly different context, of "intendimento" with the notion of body. To be
sure, in xxv it is the "body" of the poem beneath its figurative
dress which harbors the poem's "verace intendimento," while
in chapter iii it was the body of Beatrice beneath a crimson veil
which harbored the "verace giudicio" of Dante's vision. But are

these not ultimately equivalent? And when Dante speaks of the denudation of a poem's figurative dress, is he not proposing an unlikely agenda in light of the "marvelous vision," where the undenudable Beatrice first disclosed the space of figuration?

What is provocative about the metaphors governing the literary theory of xxv is not only their inadvertent relay to chapter III but also that Dante has recourse to figurative language at precisely the moment he presumes to contain it in a series of academic and technical categories: substance and accident, meaning and expression, reason and rhetoric, etc. This fall back into the figurative is no accident. It reveals a profound irony in Dante's call for the prosaic denudation of poetic dress. Dante's ostensible denudation of the figure of the lord is fraught with these same ironies, for while he announces that the legitimate employment of a figure of speech allows him to represent love as a *corporeal* substance, the truth is that the person of Beatrice has at this point substantialized love and rendered the lord an illegitimate figure. Dante is in some sense forced to expel him from the narrative, to denude his figure and do away with it. Henceforth it is the person of Beatrice which legitimates poetic personification; indeed, it is Beatrice who authenticates all figurative speech that desires to praise her, or that arises from the animation of her presence. Beatrice is not an accident spoken of as a substance by virtue of a poetic license; nor is she merely the opposite of this; rather, she is the very source of that license which permits Dante to speak in that manner by which he is inspired. The desire for communication with the beloved which lies at the origin of vernacular poetry becomes the event of Beatrice's communication to Dante of the poetic license that enables him to speak in praise of her.

Dante has introduced a set of distinctions in xxv. Love is not a "corporeal substance" but an accident. The "meaning" of a poem does not lie in its veils of figures and "rhetorical color," but in the logic that underlies the *vesta di figura* and makes the poem a coherent deployment of figurative language. The good poets distinguish themselves from the bad by their ability to "denude" their poems of the figurative dress and to expose the *intendimento* in prose.

Now, to speak of figurative language as dress and exterior guise, in other words, as a *veil*, is a commonplace in Dante's literary world. In *Convivio* the "veils" of Dante's *canzoni* are stripped away systematically by the autohermeneutic, authorial exercises of allegorical interpretation. But precisely because they appear as allegories can the *Convivio*'s poems be stripped of their rhetoricity and the *verace intendimento* be exposed, for allegory always appears as a veil of tropological and catachrestic language that overlays some *other* significance.[12] Thus in *Inferno* IX, when the allegorical import of the poem is particularly crucial, the author enjoins his reader to "mira[re] la dottrina che s'asconde / sotto 'l velame de li versi strani" (LL. 62–63) ["observe the teaching that is hidden here / beneath the veil of verses so obscure"]. Allegory, in short, is always an allegory of the break between intention and expression, between the letter and its spirit; hence it is also always ironic.[13]

The body of Beatrice, on the other hand—the otherness of its unaccountable presence, of its hypostatic density, both in itself and in its incorporation in the poem—resists the allegorical compound of signification altogether. Nothing could be more antithetical to allegory than the person of Beatrice, whose body is indissociable from the phenomenal guises through which she gives herself to perception and poetic figuration.[14] It is this unity, once again, that makes her "miraculous." This holding together of the difference between her body and her guises without collapsing that difference makes her the locus of a singular presence:

> Questa gentilissima donna . . . venne in tanta grazia de
> le genti, che quando passava per via, le persone cor-
> reano per vedere lei; onde mirabile letizia me ne giun-
> gea. E quando ella fosse presso d'alcuno, tanta ones-
> tade giungea nel cuore di quello, che non ardia di

levare li occhi, né di rispondere a lo suo saluto; e di
questo molti, sì come esperti, mi potrebbero testimo-
niare a chi non lo credesse. Ella coronata e vestita
d'umiltade s'andava, nulla gloria mostrando di ciò
ch'ella vedea e udia. . . . Io dico ch'ella si mostrava sì
gentile e sì piena di tutti li piaceri, che quelli che la
miravano comprendeano in loro una dolcezza onesta e
soave, tanto che ridicere non lo sapeano; né alcuno era
lo quale potesse mirare lei, che nel principio nol con-
venisse sospirare. Queste e più mirabili cose da lei pro-
cedeano virtuosamente. (xxvi, 1–2)

This most gentle lady . . . came with such grace among
people that when she passed by they would run to see
her, which gave me much happiness. And when she
was near to someone, such honesty overtook his heart
that he would not dare raise his eyes, nor respond to
her greeting; and of this many could testify for me.
Crowned and dressed with humility, she passed by
showing no glory in what she heard and saw. . . . I say
that she showed herself so gentle and so full of grace
that those who looked on her experienced a pure and
soave sweetness which they could not express; nor
could anyone look at her without sighing. This and
more miraculous things issued forth from her virtu-
ously.

This prosaic amplification of the "Tanto gentile" sonnet in
xxvi, immediately following the digression in xxv, resumes the
hyperbolic celebration of Beatrice in Christological terms. She
has become an ontological event. The advent of her beauty
now commits a noumenal truth to the phenomenal world, and
visual perception becomes an agency of revelation. But if Beatrice appears as the locus of a revelation, her appearance also
conceals a noumenal secret. Inversions and antitheses in
Dante's language stress the very paradox of her being: she is

wondrous to look at, yet eyes turn away from her; she is an apparition showing forth a miracle ("una cosa venuta / da cielo in terra a miracol mostrare"), yet she does not show any glory in herself ("nulla gloria mostrando"). Her *umiltade*, or humility, implies the very modesty of being dressed, of withholding something from the world, and hence of refusing ostention. Beatrice's appearance, in other words, remains a vestment that reveals and also conceals her nature. In short, she gives herself to the world as she gave herself to Dante in the "marvelous vision": through so many versions of the crimson cloth veiling her body. The body of those poems that praise her through an incorporation can no more easily be laid bare than the withdrawing body of Beatrice in Dante's dream.

And yet in chapter xxv Dante calls for the prosaic denudation of poetic speech, implicitly promoting the prosimetrum practice of the *Vita Nuova* as a response to such a call. But doesn't the theory of prosaic denudation layed out in xxv remain at odds with Dante's practice throughout the work? Indeed, Dante's prosaic practice in the *Vita Nuova* in no way conforms to the agenda of "denudation" called for by chapter xxv.[15] The digression into literary theory is exceptional in the deep sense of the word, for it not only interrupts the narrative but also contradicts the deepest intention of its enterprise. Except for the deliberate decomposition of the lord of love, nowhere does Dante engage in the systematic divestment of figurative language which he recommends in chapter xxv.[16] Yet he would have us believe that in his prose, and especially in the *divisioni*, or subdivisions of his poems, he is actually laying bare the poems' "true meaning." Dante is quite explicit about the function of these *divisioni*: they divest the poems of their poetic dress. What are these *divisioni*, and do they really perform such a function?

The *divisioni* usually come after a poem and break it up into its locutionary units. A typical example following the poem "Tutti li miei penser" in chapter xiii:

This sonnet can be divided into four parts: in the first
I say and suppose that all my thoughts are of love; in
the second I say they are different, and I narrate their
difference; in the third I say that all seem in accord;
in the fourth I say that, wanting to speak of love, I
do not know from what side to seize the matter, and if
I want to seize it from them all, I must call my enemy,
namely my lady of Mercy; and I say "my lady" in an
almost disdainful way. The second part starts here:
and they have in them; and the third here: *and alone
they agree*; the fourth here: *Wherefore I do not know*.
(XIII, 10)

Through the centuries the *divisioni* have struck readers as a
dreary exercise in futility, marring the beauty of the work as a
whole. Boccaccio, for instance, eliminated them altogether
from his edition of the *Vita Nuova*. Nor do they appear in the
editio princeps of 1576. Later, Dante Gabrielle Rossetti was so
bothered by them that he left them to his brother to translate
when he labored on his famous English translation of the *Vita
Nuova*. Dante critics have tried to account for them in more or
less convincing terms. Pio Rajna was the first to link them to
the protocol of Scholastic *expositio*, which breaks up the parts of
the argument; Panofsky, in his study of Gothic architecture
and medieval Scholasticism, found them typical of the Gothic
architechtonic; in our own day a critic like Mark Musa can still
wonder whether Dante was not interested in the abstract act of
subdividing for subdividing's sake, since the sum of all other
explanations seems so unsatisfactory.[17]

But while readers have noticed their obtrusive presence,
the fact that the *divisioni* in no way fulfill their ostensible function has not been sufficiently pondered. Consider another typical *divisione* following the poem "Voi che portate" in chapter
XXII: "This poem is divided in two parts: in the first I call and
ask these ladies if they are coming from her [Beatrice], telling

them that I think so, since they return almost ennobled; in the second I beg them to tell me of her. The second part begins here: *And if you come*" (xxii, 11). On no account could this technical synopsis be called a denudation of the poem's "figurative dress" or an "opening up" of the legitimating *intendimento*. Nor do the other *divisioni* come closer to decomposing the poems' rhetoricity or figures of speech. Such denudation simply does not take place in the work, with the sole exception, once again, of the lord, whose veils of personification are stripped away by Dante only after love's absolute transference to, and dissolution in, the person of Beatrice.

Is it by chance that Dante refuses to divide the first poem after the digression in xxv? Is it also by chance that xxv falls between the two chapters which hypostasize Beatrice to an extreme? Perhaps not, but it seems that in any case we are left with an ironic contradiction between the theory proposed in xxv and the inner impulse of Dante's lyric vocation. It also seems that the author does not control this irony in any rigorous sense, which makes it all the more relevant, not to say revelatory. The artifact slips away from him. It does so at the very moment he steps outside of it to digress into literary issues in a gesture of homage to his older friend Guido—a gesture that involves more than homage, as we will see in the following chapter.

The suggestion that Dante's artifact slips away from him the moment he presumes to circumscribe it theoretically is bound to create some uneasiness. In the realm of traditional Dante scholarship, at least, the operative principle is that Dante retains a sovereign authority over the meaning of his text. Historically for this scholarship, meaning and authorial intention coincide more absolutely than perhaps with any other author in the literary canon. Dante of course went to great lengths in all his works to claim an extravagant authority for his authorship, embedding within those works a set of hermeneutic guidelines for their interpretation. Chapter xxv is only one example of this authorial legislation with regard to the hermeneutics of the work. There is no question that Dante's legislation in this domain has been remarkably successful, for still today Dantology continues its long tradition of reading Dante within the hermeneutical frameworks that he himself placed around his works. Perhaps more than any other author in history, Dante inspires such "faith" in his readers—not religious faith per se, but faith in the supreme artifactuality of the artifact.

In the case of the *Vita Nuova* such faith risks perpetuating the ambiguities or misunderstandings that characterize the author's conception of his own enterprise. One of the problems is that the real author here is not Dante at all but Beatrice, by which I mean that she generates and also authorizes the speech about her. And the *Vita Nuova* is, after all, a book about Beatrice. The question of the provenance of the voice is central to the ironic parenthesis opened and closed by xxv, for while Dante in that chapter affirms the poet's sovereignty over the *intendimento* of his poem, his lyric experience of inspiration shows that the poem has a transcendent genesis in Beatrice.

The questions of tropes, animation, and the poetic voice have reemerged in another context in recent debates among literary critics about figurative language and the lyric poem, and a brief review of those debates reveals how much is at stake in Dante's ironic digression in xxv. It was originally Eugenio Donato's and Paul de Man's rereading of the Romantic problematic that led to a revision of new-critical conceptions of the lyric poem. These conceptions were or are characterized by a neglect of the various instabilities that figures of speech introduce into the lyric poem. As Jonathan Culler points out in a panoramic essay on post-new-critical theories of lyric poetry, the new-critical view of the lyric is summarized by Northrop Frye's declaration that the lyric poem is "preeminently the utterance that is overheard."[18] Culler argues that the "figural" approach of de Man and de Manians calls into question the basis or plausibility of this fiction of a monologic lyric voice. It does so by focusing on the enabling role of tropes that pervade the

lyric poem, tropes such as apostrophe, personification, prosopopoeia—in short, tropes that subvert or reverse the distinction
between animate and inanimate things.[19]

Apostrophe, for instance (which introduces an addressee
for the speaking voice), and personification (which creates another animate presence in the poem) clearly disrupt the fiction
that, as readers, we are overhearing the private utterance of a
voice speaking to itself. The intrusion of some other animate
presence in the poem through tropological transference allows
Paul de Man to suggest that what we have in the lyric is "the
mimesis [not] of a signifier but of a specific figure, prosopopoeia."[20] Prosopopoeia is the discrete figure that gives voice to
the voiceless and face to the faceless, animating an inanimate
entity—Shelley's west wind, for instance, or Dante's lord of
love. It is a figure that for the most part anthropomorphizes.
The frequency of its deployment in the lyric undermines the
primacy of the poem's descriptive project and becomes the in-
scriptive figure that frames the lyric utterance, enabling the
voice to constitute itself as a poetic subjectivity.[21]

De Man's persuasive argument for the enabling role of prosopopoeia carries with it an entirely new problematic of the relation between voice and animation. The transference of its
own voice to inanimate things, which in turn are animated
with a mysterious speech and life of their own, leaves the lyric
subject speechless and deathlike—at the edge of its own finitude, as it were. Along with the transference of life and voice,
prosopopoeia means an evacuation of the poet's vitality, a lyric
kenosis. This explains the recurrence, in lyric poetry, of a rhetorical situation in which the poet longs for animation from the
same impersonal forces that he or she initially endowed with
life through personification or prosopopoeia.[22] The transference of the voice and the subsequent longing for reanimation
become in this way the great inner obsession of the lyric. In
other words, the tropological constitution of lyric subjectivity
creates a drama of lyric expropriation which takes place

through the discrete yet pervasive deployment of figures of speech.

The problematic that figuralist critics uncover in the Romantic lyric tradition lies at the core of Dante's digression in xxv.[23] But Dante's digression remains ironic, for while it authorializes the poetic subject, the *libello* as a whole points to a different provenance of the voice. It is well known that Beatrice never speaks in the *Vita Nuova*. What can this silence mean? It cannot mean that the author reduces her to the status of a passive object around which an active speech may accumulate its poetic figures and courtly ideologies; on the contrary, the silence of Beatrice conceals the power of animation that gives life to the voice. Her own inscrutable life is transferred over to the new life of the voice through a lyric incorporation. Before this voice can personify inanimate forces through tropological transference, it must first receive its own transcendent animation from the person of Beatrice. It is in this respect that we can say that Beatrice's silent being in the world becomes the author of the new life.

Perhaps the most revealing aspect of Dante's digression in xxv is Beatrice's total absence. In her stead we find the "first friend" Guido Cavalcanti. This is hardly by chance, for the irony and unresolved tension I have tried to disclose stem ultimately from the opposing claims of love and friendship. Chapter xxv is above all Dante's dialogue with a poet who, perhaps more than any other in literary history, experienced the instabilities of figurative language as a deep personal drama, and who brought the figure of personification to such an extreme in his poetry as to liquidate the very notion of personhood. The Cavalcantian drama that Dante responds to in xxv, however implicitly, is that of an exile—exile from a source of authentification for figurative speech and representation in general. Exile, in other words, from Beatrice. We have seen that Dante implicates Guido in his hypostasis of Beatrice in chapter xxiv. By evoking the figure of Giovanna, who had been Guido's lady, and linking her analogically to St. John the Baptist, Dante not only exalts Beatrice but responds to Guido's despair of an authentic representation of love. But Dante's response is pervaded by ambiguities. For some reason Guido haunts the *Vita Nuova* as a whole, and he will continue to haunt Dante's poetic enterprise up until the very end of the *Commedia*. Who is Guido Cavalcanti and why do we not know more about him?

4 The Ghost of Guido Cavalcanti

Sister Sonnets: Guido Cavalcanti is one of the most re-
Breath and Death markable poets who ever put pen to paper, and Dante knew it. Their friend-
ship is also one of the more thought-provoking episodes of
literary history. We cannot presume to comprehend the initial
impulse of Dante's career without confronting the tensions of
this friendship; nor will we get very far with the *Vita Nuova*
without uncovering the recesses haunted by the ghost of
Cavalcanti.

There are many reasons to speak of the ghost of Cavalcanti, or better, to speak of Cavalcanti as a ghost. To begin
with, he was deeply haunted by the immanence of his own
death, by the self's ontological insubstantiality, and by the failures of representation to reach the other side of finitude. The
whole range of conventions and *topoi* of medieval lyricism—
from the courtly poetry of Provence and Sicily to the municipal
moralism of Guittone d'Arezzo to the professorial stilnovism of
Guinizelli—gets reduced in Guido's corpus to an obsessive psychic drama of subjective expropriation and fragmentation. The
dazzling technical intricacies of his poems merely repeat the
complex science whereby the lonely psyche processes its experiential data only to find itself overwhelmed and undone by the
sheer excess of the world.[1] These psychic processes, which medieval Aristotelian psychology theorized and systematized in
various versions, constitute the essential thematic material of
Guido's *Canzoniere*. Not love, but the psychic mechanisms that
love puts into motion; not beauty, but the resonances of its effects on the inward vulnerability of the beholder; not joy, long-

ing, and melancholy, but the phenomenology of such emotions in the depths of the imagination—these are the psychic phenomena that become the focus of a poetry that singlehandedly rewrites the lyric tradition in terms of a radical phantasmology of the self.[2]

Before looking at how the ghost of Guido Cavalcanti haunts Dante's corpus, I will discuss some examples of the haunted nature of Guido's own verse. I begin with the sonnet "Chi è questa che ven," not because it represents an extreme example of Guido's phantasmology—it in fact does not—but because it appears as a "sister" to Dante's "Tanto gentile," which I have already dwelled upon at some length. An analysis of Guido's poem in relation to "Tanto gentile" will serve to introduce some of the essential differences, difficulties, and disruptions that characterized the poets' friendship. It is not known which sonnet was written first, nor does it ultimately matter.

> Chi è questa che vèn, ch'ogn'om la mira,
> e fa tremar di chiaritate l'âre,
> e mena seco Amor, sì che parlare
> null'omo pote, ma ciascun sospira?
>
> O Deo che sembra quando li occhi gira
> dical'Amor, ch'i' nol savria contare:
> cotanto d'umiltà donna mi pare
> che ogn' altra inver' di leì la chiam' ira.
>
> Non si porìa contar la sua piagenza,
> ch'a le' s'inchin' ogni gentil vertute,
> e la beltate per sua dea la mostra.
>
> Non fu sì alta già la mente nostra,
> e non si pose in noi tanta salute,
> che propriamente n'avriàn canoscenza. (iv)

> Who is she who comes, that everyone looks at her,
> Who makes the air tremble with clarity

And brings Love with her, so that no one
Can speak, though everyone sighs?

O God, what she looks like when she turns her eyes
Let Love say, for I could not describe it.
To me she seems so much a lady of good will
That any other, in comparison to her, I call vexation.

One could not describe her gracefulness,
for every noble virtue inclines toward her
And beauty displays her as its goddess.

Our mind was never so lofty
And never was such beatitude granted us
That we could really have knowledge of her.

The scene in both poems is identical: a wondrous lady passes by like a drift of divine light, bringing the world to a rapturous halt, silencing her spectators, and causing the soul to sigh. Guido's poem figures as a poem of praise, to be sure, but also as much more. It begins with one of the most perfect stanzas of Occidental lyric poetry. The explosive advent of an unidentified lady generates an accelerated heartbeat in the nervous syncopation of the opening verses; the trembling of the air with clarity (here, too, *claritas*) gives a diffuse visual image of the inward fluttering of the heart. She paralyzes the speech of each man, the phrase *null'omo* at once individuating and nullifying the observing subject, and the verb *sospira* recalls the rhyme word *mira* as the direct cause of its expiration. Furthermore, the whole stanza is articulated as an interrogation: who is this one who comes?[3] She comes from nowhere, sudden and nameless, as an unanswered and overwhelming question. The essence of the aesthetic moment is expressed not so much in the phenomenology of beauty's effects as in the interrogative.[4] The epiphany of this nameless woman engenders a crisis brought on by the failure to identify the phenomenon that invades the sphere of perception. The essence and intensity of the aesthetic moment figure as a question about the provenance of beauty, a question that throws the observer back onto his incapacity to account for beauty's advent or to seize the inaccessible origin from which it emerges and into which it recedes with its passage. The sigh that ends the interrogative of the first stanza signals the failure of a positive response.

The lady comes and in her coming she passes. Already by the second stanza she is passing by, for it seems that she turns her eyes around in a glance: "quando li occhi gira." This swift glance of the beautiful, returning the beholder's gaze, aggravates his turmoil and initiates the poem's explicit reflection on the mind's inability to account for the experience. The remainder of the poem sustains the reflection by serializing a host of negative qualifications about the cognitive power to represent the aesthetic event: "ch'i' no 'l savria contare"; "Non si porìa contar la sua piagenza"; "Non fu sì alta già la mente nostra"; "non si pose in noi tanta salute." If in the first stanza the lady is coming, and in the second she is going, by the third stanza she has already become a memory, a remote occurrence that still troubles the reflective mind. By the last stanza her withdrawal has become absolute, for the mind has now completely turned in upon itself in a discouraged confrontation with its own cognitive impotence.

I have heard more than one *dantista* remark that Dante's superiority over Guido as a poet can be gauged by comparing the sister sonnets. Guido's begins with an explosive eruption of perfect verse, which the rest of the poem cannot sustain. The sigh comes too quickly, the lady vanishes too suddenly, and the poem features an extended anticlimax from the second stanza on. Dante's sonnet, on the other hand, embodies a slow and pneumonic intake of poetic breath which allows the final sigh to come as the climactic release of the poem's inspiration. While this is true, on no account can we take Dante's sonnet as the exemplary measure that Guido's falls short of in its version of an aesthetic epiphany. A radical divergence of poetics and ideology is at stake. As for the question of comparable poetic virtuosity, there is no doubt that Guido is essentially the more accomplished lyric poet. However, the issue is not one of technical virtuosity but, once again, of divergent agenda sustained by divergent ideologies. For Dante the beauty of Beatrice gives rise to aesthetic placation; for Guido the phenomenon of beauty troubles, excites, and disquiets the subject by dramatizing his exile from its remote provenance. In Dante's sonnet the beholder gives himself over to the sanctifying presence of Beatrice, finding in her otherness an event of grace which liberates him from the very confines of subjectivity (Beatrice *greets* others—"ella altrui saluta"—hence she saves them from their otherness). In Guido's sonnet, on the other hand, the mysterious lady vanishes as suddenly as she appears, with an elusive glance that condemns others to their otherness from her; thus the penultimate verse, "e non si pose in noi tanta *salute*," seals the "we" off from the lady and disclaims any hope for a substantial event of grace such as the one celebrated by Dante in "Tanto gentile."

An irreducible difference of vision, then, underlies these comparable sonnets. No less accomplished than Dante's, Guido's moves deliberately in an opposite direction: from exterior to interior, from grace to disgrace, from liberation to confinement, from transcendence to finitude. Its subject retreats into the isolated recesses of subjectivity, where it confronts its failure to reappropriate the beautiful through its powers of representation. The beautiful comes from afar and throws the world into disarray, for it is not *of* this world, and the beholder who stays behind strains at the limits of his finite subjectivity, limits that, once again, figure as so many epistemological inadequacies ("n'aviam canoscenza," etc.). In short, while in Guido's poem the transcendent exteriority of beauty promises an alternative to the beholder's finitude, the inarrestable passage of the aesthetic phenomenon as well as its resistance to representation only serve to disclose the abyss of finitude even further. There are substantial reasons, therefore, why the sigh comes "too early" in Guido's sonnet. Guido refuses or despairs of incorporation. While the climactic sigh in "Tanto gentile" initiates a process of recuperation and incorporation whereby the poem rises to the occasion of Beatrice's presence, the sigh in Guido's poem initiates a descent into the haunted interiority of the solitary psyche. It seems so clear, in retrospect, that it was Dante's destiny to become the poet of ascent. But his older friend remains in every respect the poet of descent; thus, he begins his sonnet at an impossible height and charts the fall from that height into subjective disgrace. Cavalcanti remains one of the most subtle poets of despair who ever wrote.[5]

The crucial question is the following: Does Dante's ascent begin where Guido's descent ends, or does Guido's descent begin where Dante's sigh closes the circle of lyric incorporation?

Personification and Personhood

What we see in "Chi è questa che ven" is only a small shadow of the Cavalcantian night. His *Canzoniere* as a whole contains numerous and extraordinarily crafted poems in the "tragic style," as it is has been called, which come together to form the portrait of a forlorn subjectivity.[6] The debate about the degree to which Guido was commited to the Averroist doctrine of the unity of the intellect and its radical separation from the material world is still open. Most of the evidence indicates that he most certainly was not un-Averroist.[7] What seems unquestionable is that much of Guido's poetry mobilizes an elaborate and abstruse psychology in which the self appears as the arena of multiple intersections of autonomous and impersonal psychic processes which reduce the self to a state of passivity with regard to experience. It has been convincingly argued that for Guido the personal subject is not a subject at all but rather the indifferent object on which a radically transcendent universal (agent) Intellect acts.[8] This state of subjective helplessness would seem to underlie the proliferation of lexical terms that pervade Guido's corpus and describe the negative emotional facticity of the lyric subject: "sbigottimento," "temenza," "dubbioso," "paura," "consumare," "distruggere," "tremare," "disfare," and so forth.[9]

It is no accident that this *vocabulorum discretio* recurs invariably in the context of love. In Guido's phantasmology the love experience serves to radicalize the self's confrontation with its own remoteness from salvation and its resignation to the claims of death. Hence Guido's consistent linking of the motifs of love and death involves a deliberate play on the isomorphic words of *Amore* and *Morte*. The specter of personal death haunts Guido's corpus as the absolute limit that forever liquidates the integrity of the self and denies any substantial access to transcendence.

Guido's doctrinal *canzone*, "Donna me prega," lays out in complex internal rhyme schemes and technically perfected stanzas the speculative vision of love as a predicament of expropriation and psychic fragmentation. The poem has excited endless exegesis, both philosophical and philological, and I will forgo an extended discussion of it here. Its intricate psychiatric schemes and abstract logic pose a fascinating challenge but invariably lead to a fetishism of this particular poem in Cavalcanti's corpus, and largely for the wrong reasons. The poeticity of the *canzone* becomes secondary to its disquisitional content, the logic of the psychology predominates over the figures that generate the poem, and the *canzone*'s intellectual rarefaction casts in the shadows the desperate emotion that underlies the utterance as a whole.[10] Scholars who face the challenge posed by the poem's resistance to interpretation neglect to ask how its ultimate unreadability *as* a poem allegorizes, as it were, the disorientation of the love experience which forms its content.[11] The emotive drive in Cavalcanti's poetry is for the most part ingeniously interwoven in a fabric of connective logical and terminological coordinates that draw attention to the elaborate production of the design itself, and in the case of "Donna me prega" this Cavalcantian artistry almost becomes extreme enough to dissimulate the pathos that informs it. I will steer clear of the *canzone*, then, and move to a more accessible and finally more typical poem of Guido's which illustrates the pat-

terns and issues that interest us here. The following poem is
number XIX of Guido's *Canzoniere*:

I' prego voi che di dolor parlate
che, per vertute di nova pietate,
non disdegn[i]ate la mia pena udire.

Davante agli occhi miei vegg'io lo core
e l'anima dolente che s'ancide,
che mor d'un colpo che li diede Amore
ed in quel punto che madonna vide.
Lo su' gentile spirito che ride,
questi è colui che mi fa sentire,
lo qual mi dice: "E' ti convien morire."

Se voi sentiste come 'l cor si dole,
dentro dal vostro cor tremereste:
ch'e[lli] mi dice sì dolci parole,
che sospirando pietà chiamereste.
E solamente voi lo 'ntendereste:
ch'altro cor non poria pensar né dire
quant' è 'l dolor che mi conven soffrire.

Lagrime ascendon de la mente mia,
sì tosto come questa donna sente,
che van faccendo per li occhi una via
per la qual passa spirito dolente,
ch'entra per li [occhi] miei sì debilmente
ch'oltra non puote color discovrire
ch 'l 'maginar vi si possa finire.

I beg of you who speak of sorrow
That, by dint of rare compassion,
You not disdain to hear my woe.

Before my eyes I see the heart
And the grieving soul that are slain,
That die from a blow that Love gave them,

And at that point when it saw my lady.
Her noble spirit that laughs
Is the very one that makes itself heard by me,
That tells me: "You will have to die."

If you could sense how the heart grieves,
Within your hearts you would tremble:
For it says to me such sweet words
That, sighing, you would invoke mercy.
And only you would understand it:
For no other heart could think or tell
How great is the sorrow I have to suffer.

Tears rise up from my mind
As soon as it senses my lady;
They make, through the eyes, a conduit
Through which passes the grieving spirit
That enters through my eyes so weakly
That it cannot reveal any color
Beyond that which imaging could complete from it.

What makes this ballad so masterful is above all the sub-
tlety and refinement of its poetic effects: the numerical asymme-
try of the rhyme scheme, the double *rime baciate* that end each
full stanza, the dense but casual assonances and alliterations,
the rhythmic control and resolution of the verses, and, finally,
the manifold rhetorical figures that create the visualization of
an invisible psychic space of sensation and susceptibility. The
first anomalous stanza appeals for audience and compassion
from those who, by nobility of heart, can identify with the poet's afflictions. The second stanza personifies the lover's heart
and soul as the slain victims of love's blows, where love figures
as yet another personification. The solecism whereby Guido
singularizes what should be the pluralized verbs *ancidere* and
videre makes of the heart and soul a single entity sharing an
identical fate. Furthermore, through a remarkable tropological
transference, this double entity is endowed with the faculty of

sight. It, or they, sees ("vide") the lady, while the actual eyes see only the heart and soul in their distraught state. The concluding tercet of the stanza shifts to the auditory faculty: here too by way of a personification, the lady's "noble spirit" appears as laughing and speaking, telling the lover "You will have to die." In addition to the figure of personification, we have also that of antithesis: the laughing spirit brings tidings not of joy but of death.

The third stanza recovers the vocative mode and conjures up the interiority of the heart ("dentro dal vostro cor") where worthy lovers should tremble as they hear how the poet's heart grieves. Here again the heart is personified and speaks "sweet words" that call for mercy from the noble hearts that have a similar sentient and vulnerable interiority. The stanza figures as a *captatio* and, like the previous one, deploys the figure of antithesis to link "sweet words" with the call for mercy.

The last stanza describes an extraordinary interference between the internal and external through the tears that overspill and blur their boundaries. The tears rise up from the mind the moment the mind feels ("sente") the lady's presence, and they spill out through the eyes. This opening of the eyes onto the world through the outpouring of tears allows the "grieving spirit," which has left the lover's body to be with the lady, to reenter the lover's body through those same eyes, bearing with it the image of the lady. But because of the tears, the image this spirit conveys is so blurred, its colors so faint, that the imagination is unable to complete ("finire") the image itself. In short, the process of perception is interrupted.

What is this poem about? If we call it a love poem we are dealing with a remarkable love poem indeed. As in so many of Cavalcanti's poems, the lady here is a wholly abstract and remote entity who serves only to trigger the process of introjection. Nor is there an irreducible subjective protagonist, a central lyric "I," who organizes the phantasmic events and gives them a center. Just as the lady is metonymically fragmented— her "noble spirit" laughing and telling the lover that he must die—so too the lover is fragmented into discrete and autonomous personified entities: the eyes, the heart and soul, the tears, the "grieving spirit," each of which becomes a protagonist in a drama that enacts itself independently of the lover's control. In fact the self is reduced here to nothing more than the stage where a series of personified figures play out a scene of psychic turmoil and despair, like uncanny actors with predetermined roles. The catharsis of tears in the last stanza comes about mechanically and inexorably, by virtue of a logic that dominates the autonomous interaction of the psychic elements. While the drama is triggered by the sight of the lady—not even by the eyes but by the heart and soul—it culminates in a flooding of the eyes that discolors and blurs her image, leaving the imagination with insufficient data to complete the image itself. Such a poem clearly revises the traditional patterns of love poetry—its *topoi*, conventions, and themes—and turns them into a psychic phenomenology that not only decomposes the subject of experience but makes of this decomposition the very matter of poetry. No poet either before or after Guido has been so radical in this respect; nor does a haunted poetics of this sort readily lend itself to imitation, though Dante was under its spell for a while.

We can already see that what is essential to Guido's poetics is a systematic and exasperated deployment of tropes, above all personification. It has been remarked that personification is the "key figure of Cavalcanti's poetry."[12] It allows for a concretion of the abstract, an abstraction of the concrete, the animation of the inanimate, and, at crucial moments, the deanimation of the animate. Love is by far the most personified entity in Guido's corpus, as it is in the *Vita Nuova*, but although the figure is a traditional one in medieval love literature, Guido's personifications give it a wholly new function within the economy of the poem, where it consistently speaks to the lover of his death. We have in Guido an explicit and deliberate dramatization of what Paul de Man identifies as the syndrome of tropological animation which leaves the poet on the brink of his own annihilation. In Guido's *Canzoniere* the figure of love is animated with speech in order to speak to the personifying subject of his own death and undoing.[13] But the trope goes even further in Guido's poetry. Through the trope's proliferation, a nuclear fragmentation of the experiential subject reveals the anonymous psychic chain reactions that disrupt the subject's cohesion. As countless personifications decompose the self into discrete and autonomous entities, the integrity of personhood itself is liquidated. Sonnet XVIII offers a dramatic version of this dissolution.

> Noi siàn le triste penne isbigotite,
> le cesoiuzze e 'l coltellin dolente,
> ch'avemo scritte dolorosamente
> quelle parole che vo' avete udite.
>
> Or vi diciàn perché noi siàn partite
> e siàn venute a voi qui di presente:
> la man che ci movea dice che sente
> cose dubbiose nel cor apparite;
>
> le quali hanno destrutto sì costui
> ed hannol posto sì presso a la morte,
> ch'altro non n'è rimaso che sospiri.
>
> Or vi preghiàn quanto possiàn più forte
> che non sdegn[i]ate di tenerci noi,
> tanto ch'un poco di pietà vi miri.

We are the poor bewildered quills,
The little scissors and the grieving penknife,
Who have sorrowfully written
Those words that you have heard.

Now we tell you why we have left
And presently come here to you:
The hand that used to move us says it feels
Dreadful things that have appeared in the heart,

Which have so undone him
And brought him so close to death
That nothing else is left of him but sighs.

Now we beg you as earnestly as we can
That you not scorn to keep us
For so long as a little compassion suits you.

Who is writing the poem? An exacerbated prosopopoeia
gives speech to the very instruments of writing, not only direct
speech to the quills, scissors, and penknife but also an indirect
and relayed speech to the hand that writes. The person ("costui") who once moved the writing hand is at the brink of death,
evacuated of all substantiality and reduced to pure spirit, to the
immaterial sighs by which his life expires. He is undone, *destrutto*; dreadful things have appeared in his heart; the hand that
once wrote is motionless; yet by virtue of an extreme transference of the voice, the impersonal utensils of his writing table
speak the case of the destroyed person, as if with the breath of
his last sighs. The ghost of the abandoned person gives a
ghostly speech to the very instruments that speak his undoing.
We are on the far side of salvation here.

**The Politics of
Friendship**   Guido's ghost haunts not only the
Cavalcantian corpus but Dante's as
well. The friendship of the two poets
came to an end shortly after the period of the *Vita Nuova*, for
reasons that have to do with political and perhaps even metaphysical differences, but it seems that Dante never managed to
come to terms with the sinister question mark that drifts
through Guido's poetry and ideology, the question mark that
accompanies every gesture of figurative representation. Even in
the *Commedia*, which exorcises almost every disquieting spirit
in its spiritual architectonic, Dante was unable to deal properly
or even honestly with the spirit of his "primo amico."[14] In the
famous canto X of the *Inferno*, the confrontation with Guido's
father is marked by spiteful equivocations, bad faith, and cun-

ning malevolence on Dante's part. It is in no way an exorcism. Here as elsewhere in the *Commedia*, Guido is present by virtue of his absence, haunting the poem with this absence.[15] In cantos XXIV and XXVI of *Purgatorio*, where Dante encounters the genealogy of vernacular poets who had a formative influence on his literary career, the most important influence of all is once again absent, an unappeased spirit lurking in the shadows of this ceremonious but largely hypocritical tribute of Dante to his vernacular predecessors. In *Purgatorio* XI, where it seems that Guido is given a place in the linear literary history that culminates with Dante himself, the articulation is likewise fraught with insidiousness: "così ha tolto l'uno a l'altro Guido / la gloria della lingua; e forse è nato / chi l'uno e l'altro caccerà dal nido" ["so has one Guido removed from the other the glory of the language; and maybe one is born who will chase one and the other from the nest"].[16]

Dante knew something about chasing Guido from his nest. In the year 1300, as a memeber of the City Council of Florence, he signed the proclamation that sent Guido, along with other leaders of the White Guelf party, into exile. Although he was allowed to return to Florence after some months, Guido had contracted a disease during his forced exile and died from it shortly thereafter, in August of 1300.

But the fact that Dante is in some way implicated in Guido's death is not the only or even the main reason Guido haunts the *Commedia*, though the ambiguity of this implication helps explain the recurrent ambiguity of Guido's absent presence in the poem. What we must understand about Dante is that when it came to father figures, he was adept at acknowledging their authority, annexing it to his own authorial claims, and then "transcending" it. In *Inferno* X, he uses Virgil as the authority figure to justify his legitimacy as a poet over Guido. Later in the poem, however, he will debunk Virgil in this capacity and expel him from the poem.[17] It is no exaggeration to say that the dynamism of the *Commedia* as a whole consists mainly of Dante's gestures of erecting and then debunking figures of authority in a relay of appeals to ever higher authorities until the pilgrim finds himself face to face with the author of all creation, the author through whom Dante's authorship of the poem is presumably authenticated. The pattern of transcendence which hyperstructures the journey relies upon this logic of sublating the various authorities of other poets, traditions, or ideologies, all of which have their place in the architectonic of salvation history. Dante scholarship in fact thrives on disclosing the countless local ways in which this pattern of sublation and transcendence operates in the poem. (What is fascinating and would require a separate investigation in itself is the conspicuous manner in which so many Dantologists share or inherit Dante's neurosis about authority. If the *Commedia* appears as a sustained and manifoldly articulated Oedipal drama in which the son successfully wins out over various father figures, Dante scholarship to a large extent rehearses the drama in the genealogy of scholars intent on claiming a proper hermeneutical authority with regard to the poem.)

The subversive aspect of Dante's relation with Guido is that it escapes containment by the Oedipal structure; thus, it escapes containment by the *Commedia*. Six or seven years older than Dante, Guido was too young to become a father figure and too old not to have a natural seniority over Dante. This seniority was also social: Dante came from a family of petty nobility, while Guido was a dashing and haughty aristocrat who belonged to an illustrious magnate family.[18] Add to this the fact that, while he was alive, Guido was the superior lyric poet—from the perspective of technique and refinement, in any case—and one begins to understand some of the reasons the Cavalcanti question remained unresolved by Dante even long after the poets had broken off their friendship. What makes the relationship interesting for literary history is the way it places a question mark on the margins of Dante's entire enterprise. One cannot be haunted by that which one has overcome; and while fathers can be overcome by sublation and substitution, the older brother cannot. At most he can be denied, rejected, refused as a model of imitation, or merely dismissed. Yet even in dismissal one neither incorporates nor does away with him. At most one reduces his existence to that of a disquieting shadow.

Although it is dedicated to Guido, the *Vita Nuova* tells an implicit story of Dante's act of independence from the "primo amico" and his discovery of the horizon of his own distinct potential as a poet. A subterranean polemic serves to distance the author from his friend's ideology and to define his project in opposition to it, so that by the end of the work Guido becomes a shadow in the background of the narrative climax. The pattern seems quite clear: in the first part of the work the poems parade an explicit Cavalcantianism, while the prose recounts the bewildering and defacing nature of the protagonist's love in the Cavalcantian vein. But a gradual yet decisive turn takes place in the narrative, beginning with Dante's decision to embrace the laudatory mode as the vocation of his lyric. We have a clear signal of Dante's distantiation from Guido in chapter xx, immediately following "Donne ch'avete." Here, as we have seen, an anonymous friend asks Dante to say what love is, much the way Orlandi had asked Guido to define the nature of love, occasioning the doctrinal *canzone* "Donna me prega" as a response. Dante, however, responds to this anonymous friend with a sonnet that falls back on the authority of Guinizelli's doctrine of the identity between love and the gentle heart. I remarked that from a literary point of view the sonnet is mediocre, but it contains a narrative signal, a gesture of distantiation, a subtle turn, for it seems deliberately to invoke the authority of Guinizelli against that of Guido.

While this is merely a signal or intimation, a decisive turn against Guido clearly takes place in chapter xxiv. In our earlier discussion of this chapter we saw that Dante here substantializes love in the person of Beatrice and expels the figure of the lord from the narrative once and for all. We recall the scene: the lord appears before Dante in his "imagination," which is where Guido locates love's proper place ("In quella parte dove

sta *memora* / prende suo stato," v. 15, "Donna me prega").
Dante then sees his best friend's lady, Giovanna, approaching
his way. Behind her is the miraculous Beatrice, who *is* the
epiphany of love. We noted that the scene marks a turn in the
protagonist's orientation, from phantasmic interiority to the
aesthetic exteriority of being in the world. What we did not
note in the earlier discussion is that Dante composes a sonnet
on this occasion addressed to Guido. Its version of the event is
identical to the prose account except for a few significant omis-
sions. Here is how Dante, in the prose, accounts for the omis-
sions:

> Onde io poi, ripensando, propuosi di scrivere per rima
> a lo mio primo amico (tacendomi certe parole le quali
> pareano da tacere), credendo io che ancor lo suo cuore
> mirasse la bieltade di questa Primavera gentile.
> (xxiv, 6–7)

> And so, thinking it over, I thought to write some
> verses for my best friend (remaining silent about cer-
> tain things that called for silence), believing that his
> heart still admired the beauty of this gentle Primavera.

The parenthesis is not as enigmatic as it promises to be: it tells
us that Dante was reluctant, in Guido's regard, to advance or
exploit the analogy of St. John the Baptist and Christ. After all,
how would Guido have reacted to an allegorized suggestion
that poetically he "comes before" and prepares the way for
Dante? Furthermore, he surely would have found the analogy
absurd, especially since, according to all evidence, it was not
Guido who gave Giovanna the *senhal* "Primavera" but rather
Dante, precisely in this poem to Guido.[19] But in Dante's prose
the lord of love claims to have inspired Guido with the *senhal*
"Primavera" for the sole sake of this occasion, when Giovanna
would precede Beatrice on the street. When Dante wrote his
sonnet he was perhaps reluctant to trouble the allegiance with
Guido, but the fact that in his prose he elaborates the analogy

between Giovanna and St. John the Baptist indicates that, in the meantime, this allegiance has taken a dubious turn. Whatever Dante remained silent about at the time comes forth in more than explicit terms now.

More provocative than Dante's parenthesis is the reason he gives in chapter xxiv for composing this poem for Guido: "credendo io che ancor lo suo cuore mirasse la bieltade di questa Primavera gentile." It informs us that, at the time, Dante was mistaken about Guido's affections. Guido no longer "admired" or "looked upon" the beauty of Giovanna at the time (mirare means both to admire and to look at). It is here, in the discrete admission of a mistake on Dante's part, that we must look for the deeper recesses of the ideological turn against Guido. What is at stake?

Quite simply, Guido's doctrine of abstraction. I give this label to the theoretical psychology of evacuation and decomposition in which Guido grounds his poetics. The psychology is for the most part technical, learned, and abstruse, and Dante adopts it at times in the Vita Nuova. When in chapter xxv Dante defines love as an "accident" occurring in "substance," he is echoing the Scholastic Aristotelian terminology of Cavalcanti's "Donna me prega." In both cases the terms are used in a technical sense, where substance refers to this or that particular entity in its particularity, and accidents to the predicates that occur in the substance but do not properly belong to it. Thanks to their accidents, substances can be identified by the mind, subsumed under generic categories, and, ultimately, spoken about as this or that entity. To identify this particular tree as a tree already involves the "accidence" (literally, the "befalling") of a universal in a substance. Now, Guido's doctrine of abstraction is founded on the principle that the ideal realm of the universals remains radically transcendent and differentiated from the world of particular and material substances. The universals have an eternal, independent existence of their own, while substances perish. In a simplified version, this seems to be the notorious Averroism to which Cavalcanti subscribed, however loosely or rigorously we cannot be sure. It seems at least clear that a doctrine of ontological divorce between these orders of reality underlies Guido's systematic poetics of decomposition. Lyricizing the language and logic of radical Aristotelian psychology, Guido evacuates substance of its accidental universals through an exasperated deployment of tropes and an acute literalization of figurative language, thus painting a picture of subjective exile from the objective and transcendent realm from which the universals befall the world of materiality. Thus, in "Donna me prega" Guido can turn into poetry the impersonal process whereby an object of perception (the lady) passes from the external to the internal senses, then from the internal senses to memory, where the image becomes a phantasm, and then from memory to the possible intellect, where the agent intellect finally *abstracts* all the particular traits from the phantasm and reduces it to its universal predicates.[20] Love will be defined by Guido as this agency of memoration whereby the phantasm crosses the line that divides the material and intellectual orders of reality and frees itself from the material substance that gave rise to the process. For these orders of reality are separated by an abyss, and when the phantasm moves from memory to its seat in the possible intellect, whatever connection it had with the original object of perception—the lady herself—gets severed.

Thus, the lover who stands speechless before a beautiful woman ("Chi è questa che ven"), or whose entire physiological and psychological constitution is disrupted by the perception of such beauty, actually experiences the tragic remoteness of the provenance of beauty (beauty, for Guido, is nothing more than an intimation of that provenance). Love figures as a dangerous confusion between the woman proper and the ineffable, ideal beauty that inheres in her corporeal substance only accidentally, that is to say, not as a proper attribute but as a condescension from another realm. Her beauty, in other words, belongs to an independent order of reality that has no *substantial* links to the world of generation and decay, and no real similitude in the world of substances ("si che non pote largir *simiglianza*," v. 28, "Donna me prega"). Hence the beautiful woman remains an evanescent and bewitching simulacrum that leads to distraction as the lover's earthly appetites are aroused and his mind loses the calm necessary for its pure contemplation of the universals.

We come back, through this circuitous route, to the question of personhood and personification. Who is Giovanna for Guido? A deceptive and ultimately evanescent simulacrum of love. Guido's despair of true similitudes in the temporal realm and his metaphysical doctrine of the impersonal character of both love and beauty underlie this unusual poetics of subjective decomposition, with its proliferations of metonymic personifications of various organs and faculties of the composing person.[21] Just as the lyric subject is tropologically liquidated in the space of the poem, so too the impersonal lady who triggers the emotional fragmentation is ultimately neutral, and hence substitutable, in her simulacrous status. But Dante, at the time he wrote his sonnet to Guido, believed that Guido still admired the beauty of his lady Giovanna: "credendo io che *ancor* lo suo cuore mirasse la bieltade di questa Primavera gentile." The semantic plasticity of the phrase—which interiorizes the contemplation of beauty in and through, but also apart from, the beautiful woman ("lo suo cuore mirasse")—as well as the subjunctive mood of the verb *mirare*, sum up the tragic outlook (inlook) of the "primo amico." Guido no longer admires the beauty of Giovanna; her spell has, for him, been broken; her beauty, which never belonged to her person as such, has revealed its remoteness from all substance; time, in other words, has revealed Giovanna's chimeric status.

Dante's invocation of Giovanna in chapter XXIV vindicates her against Guido's despair of authentic personhood. It is in this chapter that Dante hyperbolically hypostasizes the person of Beatrice on the basis of her substantial *similitude* to love: "E chi volesse sottilmente considerare, quella Beatrice chiamerebbe Amore, per molta *simiglianza* che ha meco" ["And whoever thinks subtly about Beatrice would call her love, because of the great similitude that she bears to me"]. As Beatrice becomes singular, substantial and hypostatic, her miraculousness makes it possible even to retrieve Giovanna from the oblivion of Guido's affections and to authenticate her person in relation to Beatrice's. A doctrine of abstraction gives way to the hyperbole of incarnation.

Dante's polemical gesture against Guido in chapter xxiv helps explain the ironic digression that follows. We saw that chapter xxv is essentially a tribute to Guido; but now it appears as if the author, having troubled the terms of the friendship, anxiously embarks upon a digression in which he reaffirms and restabilizes his poetic allegiance to Guido. To embark in this case means to recover the spirit of marine friendship expressed in Dante's early sonnet "Guido 'i vorrei," and once again to *ragionar d'amore* among friends. Furthermore, the desire to reassure Guido, or to mitigate the gesture of distantiation from him, also seems to account for the distorted literary theory advanced in the digression: a theory of prosaic decomposition that suits Guido's poetics far more than Dante's. The digression, however, is precisely that—a digression—for the narrative picks up in chapter xxvi exactly where it left off: at the height of Beatrice's incarnational glory.

The *Vita Nuova* contains one last direct mention of Guido in chapter xxx, after which he becomes a ghost that the narrative will try to exorcise from its new life. One form this exorcism takes is the attempt at substitution. We owe to Rachel Jacoff the insight that Dante's invocation of Beatrice's brother in chapter xxxii marks an attempt to substitute Guido in his role as friend. Dante describes this new character as "amico a me immediatamente dopo lo primo" ["friend to me immediately after the first"]. As Jacoff points out, the naming of the new friend is "a circumlocution which nevertheless calls attention to the shift in allegiance."[22]

The ghost of Cavalcanti is never wholly exorcised, however; not from the *Vita Nuova*, where a Cavalcantian drama returns toward the end of the narrative; or in *De vulgari elo-quentia*, where Dante celebrates Cino da Pistoia over Guido and, by scarcely mentioning the "primo amico," gives him a ghostly presence; or certainly in the *Convivio*, where Dante is closer to Guido's poetics and ideology than ever; and not yet in the *Commedia*, where Guido's absent presence haunts a text that otherwise exorcises every possible phantom through its architectonic of representation and figuration. This much seems certain: that Guido and Dante were from the very beginning different in their ideological, social, and poetic identities. As the younger brother figure in the friendship, Dante had anxieties about articulating their differences and entering into his own "poetential," as it were. Indeed, Dante had an unusual and inordinate anxiety about differences in general. He could not have become the greatest synthetic poet in history had he been more relaxed about difference. He simply could not deal with differences except by ideologizing them. In his case this meant mobilizing a great vision of totality—a principle of identity—which neutralizes the difference in differences through the architectonic of global history. But Guido remains the difference that the architectonic cannot contain. He is the ghost of analysis which drifts as a question mark on either side of the great synthetic activity of figurative representation.

PART TWO

BEATRICE DEAD

5 The Death of Beatrice and the Petrarchan Alternative

In the second part of this investigation we move from Beatrice's presence to her absence, from the poem of praise to elegy, and ultimately from lyric to narrative temporality. The articulation of the *libello*'s "story" is based upon these transitions or "intrigues" provoked by the sudden death of Beatrice. Until this point we have not had occasion to follow the story line in a systematic or diachronic manner. The reason is quite simple: Dante discovers the literary alternative of narrative only after the disappearance of Beatrice. While she lived, he experienced the plenitude of time not diachronically but holistically, as it were, in the moment of epiphanic plenitude. But Beatrice's death reveals the degree to which her presence belonged to a larger linear extension. As presence gives way to absence, the substantial dynamism of her existence becomes apparent, and a new dimension of time opens up.

What I set out to demonstrate in the second part of this investigation is that the *Vita Nuova*, considered in its totality, is nothing more—or less—than a testimony of Dante's discovery of this other dimension of time. The discovery precedes the *libello*'s status as an autobiographical narrative, for the narrative order assumed by this testimony depends upon that prior discovery. But within the parameters of the "story," the discovery or breakthrough occurs only at the end of the work. So on the one hand the *Vita Nuova* presents itself as a posthumous artifact, yet at the same time it presents itself as a "provisionary" one. I mean *provisionary* in two senses: first, in the sense of "temporary," insofar as the *libello* ends with a declaration of authorial inadequacy and an announcement to the effect that the book we have just finished reading is a provisional one, that is, a booklet "for the time being" until the author is in a position to write the genuine book about Beatrice. Second, *provisionary* means "forward looking": pro-vision. This means more than that Dante looks forward to a project for the future at the end of his *libello*; it means that the new order of temporality beyond lyric holism is in its very essence pervaded by futurity. What emerges at the end of the work is the projective if not prophetic character of being in time, which attends upon the future as the ultimate source of "meaning." The *Vita Nuova* is written or recollected forward; its memory is futural; the breakthrough that brings the narrative to an end marks the beginning of what later becomes a familiar pattern of prophetic narrative closure. But however familar that pattern is to readers of Dante's mature work, the early work harbors the secret of this provisionary relationship to time which sustains Dante's career as a whole. The story of the new life has not yet reached its end, in fact, it has barely begun, but by virtue of a projection toward its outstanding terminal point, it gains a trajectory that assures it its narrative and prophetic character. Expressed otherwise, the *Vita Nuova* tells the story not of its protagonist becoming its author but of the new life becoming a story in the first place.

The burden of part two, then, is to read Dante's narrative, from the death of Beatrice to the "miraculous vision" of the last chapter, as a story of the genesis of narrative possibility. Both the story of this genesis and its consequences are contained in the work's prose, not in its poetry. If the poems form part of the "story," it is only by virtue of their recuperation by the prose; while the poems exist for the most part as relics of a transcended past, the prose is pregnant with futurity. This distinction cannot be overemphasized. We have seen how Dante's ideal lyric crystallizes, encapsulates, or maximizes the plenitude of Beatrice's presence, forming what I have called a lyric circle of incorporation. The prose dimension of the work, on the other hand, is radically progressive and configurational. In this respect it remains antithetical to the holism of the lyric. Antagonistic temporalities come together and intersect one another in the space of the text, with a decisive triumph of narrative over lyric time. The degree to which the lyric flourished in the sphere of Beatrice's presence is the degree to which it comes to grief in her absence. It is her absence that precipitates a transcendence of the lyric confines.

Critics have noticed the tension between the poetic and prosaic dimensions of the *libello*, but their approach has been for the most part generic rather than ontological. While I too am concerned with the schizoid nature of its genre, my deeper concern is to undertake an ontology of genre in the *libello* in order to arrive at both the existential and the ideological grounds that determine in advance Dante's options with regard to literary alternatives. Essentially I agree with Edoardo Sanguineti's thesis that the *Vita Nuova* as a whole embodies "a will to prose . . . as a will to delyricization."[1] But for Sanguineti, Dante's option for prose is the "fruit of a calculated rhetorical research." What I try to show here is that, prior to any rhetorical research, the option for prose is first given or opened up by a rupture in the schema of time; that behind the rhetorical choice lies an existential *prise de conscience*; and that narrative figures not so much as a result of rhetorical considerations but as a result of Dante's consequential vision of time's extensions. In short, narrative as the result of a "miraculous" vision. These remarks are of course proleptic and will be expanded upon throughout this second part.[2]

In this opening chapter of part two I deal at length with the poetics of Petrarch. The reason has to do with the way Petrarch represents an option that Dante confronts and then repudiates after the death of Beatrice. Petrarch here represents a poet who takes the lyric enterprise to a certain paradigmatic extreme from the perspective of which we can better perceive what is at stake in Dante's decision to revise his lyric ambitions. Earlier in this study I remarked that Dante, Cavalcanti, and Petrarch form a trinity that paradigmatically represents late medieval lyric alternatives. I also observed that Dante brings the Cavalcantian and Petrarchan alternatives together within the space of the *Vita Nuova* in order to dramatize his option for another literary alternative altogether. Having examined the case of Cavalcanti at the end of part one, we will begin part two by examining a case of lyric stubbornness—of lyric heroism or holism—which in its own way represents a counter-alternative to the one Dante embraces by the end of the *Vita Nuova*.

One more preliminary remark: I included the discussion of Cavalcanti in part one and turn to Petrarch in part two because the lyric agenda of Dante and Cavalcanti diverge most radically in their ideologies of presence. While for Dante the transcendent exteriority of Beatrice remained an experience of grace, for Guido the epiphany of beauty amounts to an experience of personal exile and disgrace. Both experiences, however, take place in the sphere of a transcendent presence, one inclusive and the other exclusive of the lyric subject. With Petrarch, the lyric agenda becomes for the most part an elegiac one, involving above all an *absence*. Withdrawing from the realm of transcendent exteriority, Petrarch seeks to constitute lyric presence from within rather than from without. Whatever the transcendence that troubled or edified Cavalcanti or Dante, it has become inaccessible or absent by the time Petrarch takes up his pen. Thus Petrarch's lyric represents in many ways the work of mourning, with all the narcissism that Freud has taught us to associate with this phenomenon. In short, what I have called the "Petrarchan alternative" becomes real for Dante only in the wake of the loss of Beatrice.[3]

The Death of Beatrice

The presence of Beatrice means a felicitous symbiosis between the lyric voice and the person of its praise. We have seen this symbiosis at work in the ideal lyric "Tanto gentile." Chapter XXVII, which immediately follows "Tanto gentile," contains an unfinished *canzone* that describes the symbiosis in question. The *canzone*, "Sì lungiamente," is all the more signifi-

cant for the "story" that we are about to follow in that it was
interrupted and left unfinished by the sudden death of Beatrice:

> Sì lungiamente m'ha tenuto Amore
> e costumato a la sua segnoria,
> che sì com'elli m'era forte in pria,
> così mi sta soave ora nel core.
> Però quando mi tolle sì 'l valore,
> che li spiriti par che fuggan via,
> allor sente la frale anima mia
> tanta dolcezza, che 'l viso ne smore,
> poi prende Amore in me tanta vertute,
> che fa li miei spiriti gir parlando,
> ed escon for chiamando
> la donna mia, per darmi più salute.
> Questo m'avvene ovunque ella mi vede,
> e sì è cosa umil, che nol si crede
>
> (xxvii, 3–5)

> For so long has love held me
> And accustomed me to his lordship
> that, grave as he was before,
> so is he now soave in my heart.
> When he takes my power away from me
> and causes my spirits to flee away,
> then my frail soul feels
> such sweetness that my face grows pale,
> and then love has such sway over me
> that it makes my spirits speak
> and they go out calling
> my lady, to give me more beatitude.
> This happens to me wherever she sees me,
> and it is a thing so humble, that it's hard to believe.

The poem describes a state of lyric bliss, of regular and easy
access to the presence of Beatrice. The poem contains several
Cavalcantian elements (personification of spirits, hypostasis of

love, etc.), but its vision of love is wholly optimistic and in that respect un-Cavalcantian.[4] Words like *lungiamente* and *costumato* point to habituation through time and obliquely anticipate the allusion to Florence as a widowed city in the next chapter of the book. Consistent with an already familiar pattern, Dante positions his "soul" on the feminine side of the conjugal relationship (in chapter II, 7, his soul was the bride in its marriage to Love: "Amore segnoreggiò la mia anima, la quale fu sì tosto a lui disponsata" ["Love lorded over my soul, which was immediately wedded to him"]). In "Sì lungiamente" Dante's frail soul seeks from Beatrice strength and reassurance, which she provides by the power of her presence: "Questo m'avvene ovunque ella mi vede."[5]

It is this state of lyric bliss that Beatrice's death explodes in one violent, sudden, and *unspeakable* moment. Its interruption of the poem gives the *canzone* the semblance of a self-contained sonnet, but the semblance is false. If it appears to be a sonnet it is only because the poem has been cut off at the limit of Beatrice's being in the world. Death brings a quick end to the viability of lyric praise. It breaks in upon the narrative and upon this poem with the suddenness of an assassination. The poem's last word is left hanging (here too Dante does not divide the poem in his customary fashion), and chapter XXVIII opens abruptly with a quote from Jeremiah's Lamentations (I.I): "Quomodo sedet sola civitas plena populo! facta est quasi vidua domina gentium."

We have no way of gauging the initial effect of this death on Dante, at least not positively, for he apprises us of the event only obliquely, referring to it in religious terms of reconciliation. Chapter XXVIII in fact has to do with three reasons why he has chosen to remain silent about the death (silence *is* the effect of the death). These reasons are curious, and all of them point to the author's inability to record the "meaning," or *sentenzia*, of the event. His first reason sends us back to the "Proem," where Dante had declared that his intention in the *libello* is to transcribe the *sentenzia* of those events he finds written in the book of memory. He falls short of that task with regard to Beatrice's death for the second and third reasons he advances for remaining silent. The second has to do with the inadequacy of his powers of speech: "non sarebbe sufficiente la mia lingua a trattare come si converebbe di ciò" ["my language would not be sufficient to treat properly of this"]. The third reason states that, even if he could treat Beatrice's death properly, to do so would mean for Dante to become the praiser of himself ("converebbe essere me laudatore di me medesmo"). This last declaration becomes less enigmatic when we recall that until this point Dante has been the praiser of Beatrice. To now disclose the *sentenzia* of Beatrice's death would reverse the relationship of praiser and praised. Praise is due to her who reveals, not to him who reads the signs. Dante cannot be the one to record the meaning of her death; rather Beatrice must somehow, through her own death, reveal the meaning of his life. This is the story the *Vita Nuova* will tell from this moment on.

Dante's silence, however, is strictly a narrative silence. Poetically his grief bursts forth belatedly in the *canzone* "Li occhi dolenti" in chapter XXXI, creating an impression for the reader that his initial silence was a consequence of the traumatic shock of presence turned to absence in one unaccountable moment.[6] But the poems of mourning constitute a different sort of speech than the one Dante has in mind in chapter XXVIII when he chooses to remain silent, for while they give voice to the deprivations of the self, they do not transcribe the *sentenzia* of Beatrice's death as such. Up until the very end of the narrative, the prose never once presumes to engage in such transcription. In these pockets of silence—there are others—we find the recesses of the unfinished dimension of the work. Where the author remains silent, there the future holds sway over the *libello*.

The Petrarchan Alternative Structurally the death of Beatrice divides the *libello*'s temporal framework into multiple dimensions. On the one hand there are the poems composed during her lifetime; on the other there are the posthumous poems. The narrative prose belongs to another order of time altogether, posthumous even to the posthumous poems. The post-posthumous temporality of the narrative is what distinguishes the *Vita Nuova* from an anthology of poems like Petrarch's *Canzoniere*, which half a century later will gather the flowers of the poet's devotion to Laura and arrange them rhetorically according to a time frame of *Laura in vita* and *Laura in morte*. Dante goes beyond the Petrarchan alternative, but first he must confront it. What is the Petrarchan alternative?

Simply expressed, the Petrarchan alternative consists in constituting lyric presence through the relentless poetic lament of absence. The absence of Laura lamented by Petrarch so variously in his *Canzoniere* figures as the absence of a presence; the presence of this absence—its effects, its moods, its despair—is by far the most recurrent motif in the anthology. In this Petrarchan framework (the adjective referring to the poet and not to the literary conventions that trace their genealogies back to him) presence is defined, constituted, or measured in relation to the speaking subject. It is the "I" who laments, who measures Laura's absence, who here and now records the fact that Laura is not here now. In Petrarch's lyric uni-verse, so to speak, presence and absence derive their measure from the perspective of the mourning voice. The horizon of the here and now which rhetorically circumscribes every poem in Petrarch's *Canzoniere* makes the anthology a monument to the lyric voice as such. While thematically presence and absence seem opposed, this apparent opposition is effectively collapsed by an *ideal present tense* in which the lyric "I" speaks and becomes the sole measure of time's extensions. Even where the poem employs past or future grammatical tenses, this ideal present tense of the speaking voice is always operative. The pronominal "I" and the famous deictics that pervade the Petrarchan corpus serve to enshrine this ideal temporality and to make it lyrically irrevocable. "Those sighs," "these woods," "this stream," "this hillside"— the sum of "shifters" that make up the linguistic landscape of

Petrarch's poem ground the poem's temporality in the place where the voice finds itself in the here and now: now beside a stream, now on a hillside, now in the depths of memory, now in despair, now paralyzed by silence.[7] In each case the shifters point first and foremost to the fact that speech is *taking place* here and now. In each case the voice brings its here and now with it to the places that trouble or please it, empower or silence it. A lyric topology is founded upon an ideal present tense of vocalization.[8]

The famous "present progressive" tense employed so frequently by Petrarch ("I' vo gridando" [128]; "I' vo pensando" [264]; "i' vo piangendo" [365], etc.) is only a version or instantiation of the ideal present tense that keeps the voice present to itself throughout the duration of its speech. The tense is unusually appropriate for Petrarch, for it prolongs the presence of the temporal "I" as that same "I" drags the here and now with it through time.[9]

In this way Petrarch's anthology refuses the sort of narrative logic which diachronically positions the poems' *enoncés* on a projective trajectory. Each poem crystallizes its own time and inhabits its own enclosed space. The *idea* of an anthology, which we owe in effect to Petrarch, offers at most only an illusory semblance of the narrative extension and diachronicity that the poems themselves exclude from their speech acts.[10] In Petrarch's anthology each poem repeats within itself the ideal temporality of the others, so that in each case the speaking voice posits itself as the referential measure for time's ecstatic dimensions. When the voice arrives at silence after the last word of the poem, the totality of time dissolves into nullity, only to be reconstituted on the same terms as the voice takes up its speech again in the poem that follows. In this respect the individual lyrics that compose the totality of Petrarch's anthology all participate in a self-same present tense, refusing the diachronic links that would abrogate their particular autonomy. The *Canzoniere* thus organizes what one could call a sublime monadology: a constellation of windowless lyrics, each of which ideally contains and repeats the totality of the constellation within itself.[11]

Through the annulation of 365 poems (and one introductory sonnet), the monadology forms a totality based on the diurnal cycle of a secular year. But annulation here means that an invisible thread holds the lyrics together, not as a principle of linear dynamism nor as a framework of temporal containment, but rather as a gathering together of holistic crystallizations of lyric time—like the days of a year, where each diurnal cycle represents a microcosm of the annual cycle. But annulation also means the partitioning of secular time into discrete units of "todays" that provide the measure for yesterday and tomorrow. Only because there is a today can there be a yesterday and a tomorrow. In the final analysis, then, the death of Laura in no way disrupts the great synchronic artifice of Petrarch's anthology; on the contrary, it allows the poet to articulate the poles of presence and absence that inform the lyric's monadic intromission of secular time.

Such intromission takes place above all in the psychic processes of memory and anticipation, articulating a temporality based on the self's finitude. Lyric time is brought under the governance of the self's relation to its own temporal extensions, and the fullness of time is experienced by Petrarch as a psychological fusion of memory and anticipation in one sublime instant of lyric self-presence.[12] Thus, the great *canzone* number 126, "Chiare, fresche, e dolci acque," describes precisely such a process of memoration and projection which engenders a blissful moment of temporal totality in the ideal present of the speaking voice. The voice speaks to the stream and woods—a landscape bearing traces of Laura's absence—and through the self's extension backward in memory and forward unto death, a breakthrough occurs in which past and future time are brought together in the flow of the poet's speech. The two stanzas quoted below follow immediately after the poet has imagined a future beyond the bounds of his own death, when Laura will come to that same place and find that he is "already dust amid the stones" ("già terra infra le pietre"). This projection unto his death brings forth from the poet's memory a phantasmal image of Laura in the same landscape where he is located:

> Da' be' rami scendea
> (dolce ne la memoria)
> una pioggia di fior sovra 'l suo grembo,
>   et ella si sedea
> umile in tanta gloria,
> coverta già de l'amoroso nembo;
>   qual fior cadea sul lembo,
> qual su le treccie bionde
> ch'oro forbito et perle
> eran quel dì a vederle,
> qual si posava in terra et qual su l'onde,
> qual con un vago errore
> girando parea dir: "Qui regna Amore."

>   Quante volte diss'io
> allor, pien di spavento:
> "Costei per fermo nacque in paradiso!"
>   Così carco d'oblio
> il divin portamento
> e 'l volto e le parole e 'l dolce riso
>   m'aveano, et sì diviso
> da l'immagine vera,
> ch'i' dicea sospirando:
> "Qui come venn'io o quando?"
> credendo esser in ciel, non là dov'era.
> Da indi in qua mi piace
> quest'erba sì ch'altrove non ò pace.

From the lovely branches was descending (sweet in memory) a rain of flowers over her bosom, and she was sitting humble in such a glory, already covered with

the loving cloud; this flower was falling on her skirt,
this one on her blond braids, which were burnished
gold and pearls to see that day; this one was coming to
rest on the ground, this one on the water, this one,
with a lovely wandering, turning about seemed to say:
"Here reigns love."

How many times did I say to myself then, full of awe:
"She was surely born in Paradise!" Her divine bearing
and her face and her words and her sweet smile had so
laden me with forgetfulness and so divided me from
the true image, that I was sighing: "How did I come
here and when?" thinking I was in heaven, not there
where I was. From then on this grass has pleased me so
that elsewhere I have no peace.[13]

The highly stylized memory of Laura under a rain of
flowers in the same spot where the poet presently finds himself
seems like a triumph of poetic memory. In truth the poet is remembering a moment of forgetfulness, when all the coordinates
of space and time were confused: " 'How did I come here and
when?' thinking I was in heaven, not there where I was." But
the memory of forgetfulness and spatial ecstasy is merely a poetic veil or enabling fiction for that which really takes place in
the poem: a localization of the voice in the utopic space of its
vocalization: "Da indi in qua *mi piace* / *quest'erba sì ch'altrove
non ò pace.*" The lyric triumph of the poem is the result not of an
emotion recollected in tranquillity but of an original act of
gathering: the collection of time's extensions into a lyric totality
in that place outside of which the poet has no peace. That
grassy (no)place is also the space of anthology.[14]

And yet the return of the repressed—diachronic time—
continuously threatens to undo the synchronic artifice of lyric
self-constitution. Here we are at the fault line of Petrarch's poetics. Secular time holds sway over the voice, dispersing each
renewed and vocally maintained moment of self-presence. Even
the ideal temporal integration of the anthology, where the

number of poems repeats the number of days in a year, cannot ward off the dispersion to which time commits lyric presence. As the poet pursues the monadic possibilities of the lyric to their limit, the poet's struggle against the temporal predicament becomes the constitutive drama of the *Canzoniere*. Thus a monadology becomes the *Rime sparse*, the dispersed rhymes, in an ironic counterpoint to the concept of anthology. The motif of "dispersed rhymes" occurs in the introductory sonnet of Petrarch's final version of his anthology.[15] The poem summarizes for Petrarch's reader both the drama and the ambition of Petrarch's lyric enterprise:

Voi ch'ascoltate in rime sparse il suono
di quei sospiri ond'io nudriva 'l core
in sul mio primo giovenile errore,
quand'era in parte altr'uom da quel ch'i' sono;

del vario stile in ch'io piango e ragiono
fra le vane speranze e 'l van dolore,
ove sia chi per prova intenda amore,
spero trovar pietà, non che perdono.

Ma ben veggio or sì come al popol tutto
favola fui gran tempo, onde sovente
di me medesmo meco mi vergogno;

et del mio vaneggiar vergogna è 'l frutto,
e 'l pentirsi, e 'l conoscer chiaramente
che quanto piace al mondo è breve sogno.

You who hear in scattered rhymes the sound
of those sighs with which I nourished my heart
during my first juvenile error,
when I was in part another man from what I am now;

for the varied style in which I weep and speak
between vain hopes and vain sorrow, where
there is anyone who understands love through
experience, I hope to find pity, not only pardon.

But now I see how for a long time
I was the talk of the crowd, for which
often I am ashamed of myself within:

and of my raving, shame is the fruit,
and repentence, and the clear knowledge
that whatever pleases in the world is a brief dream.

In another context, one could discuss the ways in which this sonnet announces the advent of modernity. Its picture of "bad faith," its foreclosure of the possibilities of what can be expected, its exasperated self-reflexivity, all usher onto the stage a modern self-conscious subject. Restricting the scope of speculation, however, we may begin by remarking that although the sonnet stages itself as a palinode of the *Canzoniere* to follow, it in fact merely rehearses the grand theme that brings the poems together: the theme of the self's dispersion. The self that speaks here seems resigned to the condition to which it is not reconciled: existential fallenness. The last tercet describes the outcome of the poet's life and of temporal life in general with evocations of postlapsarian finitude. The allusions to Genesis in the motifs of fruit, shame, and knowledge culminate in a final statement about the ontological insubstantiality and transience of all things. No alternative is evoked. The unredeemed vanity of secular time, with all its linear dispersions, brings the poet's horizon to closure.

It is a horizon that we could describe as the space of a failed conversion. The failed conversion is alluded to and summed up in the last verse of the first stanza: "quand'era in parte altr'uom da quel ch'i' sono." On the surface of it, the adjacency of the past and present tenses of the copulas sets up a relation of alterity between the self that was and the self that now is. This alterity—"altr'uom"—would even seem to conform to the conversional logic whereby the reborn self appears severed or liberated from the old self (the case of Paul or Augustine), but this logic is undercut by the words *in parte*. In the realm of conversion such things are like pregnancy: one cannot convert in part any more than one can be partly pregnant. *In parte* here means that the poet remains committed to the errancy of his "vaneggiar," and that he is in part different but in part the same man as before. It means also that secular time *partitions* the lyric self and condemns it to a fate reflected in *Rime sparse*. Above all it means the recurrence of the partitioning that has produced the "vario stile" in which the poet weeps and speaks.[16]

We could say, then, that the rhetorical drama of the *Rime sparse* involves the *Secreto conflitu curarum mearum*. This is the complete title of one of Petrarch's confessional works, composed in Latin, which deals with his moral failure to follow the conversional itinerary of his mentor St. Augustine, with whom he is in dialogue in the work. The failure stems from the poet's excessive "self-love," which emerges as the capital vice that condemns him to the vanity of secular time and to the laurel crown's worldly fame.[17] On the other side of self-love lies conversion, the impossible virtue of the self's extension beyond itself toward the otherness of some transcendent, supratemporal term. Falling short of an act of conversion, yet despairing of existential finitude, Petrarch in the *Secreto conflitu curarum mearum* makes the same confession we hear in the lyric plaints of the *Rime sparse*, the confession of the self's *secretum*. But what is a *secretum*? When Petrarch abbreviated the full title of his work and called it merely *Secretum*, perhaps he was reacting to a tautology in the original title. A *secretum*, after all, is a *conflictus* (and a *conflictio*) insofar as *scernere*, from which the substantive derives, means to divide, distinguish, partition, separate. Petrarch's secret is simply the state of the self that, inwardly divided, struggles against itself.[18]

The *Canzoniere* is a confession of precisely this secret (the secret, once again, of modernity). The lyric self remains divided, or conflicted, between its desire for peace (which the poet prays for in the last poem) and its failure to will an event of conversion, which would grant existential time a more stable measure than it derives from the ideal temporality of the speaking voice. This, in any case, would seem to govern the logic of

Petrarch's rhetoric. We must always distinguish, of course, between the rhetoric and the performance of a Petrarchan lyric. In fact, the essence of Petrarchism may well lie in the resources and artifices by which this distinction operates.[19] In "Voi ch'ascoltate" we can see how, behind the rhetoric of resignation and lament, the rhetoric of vanity and dispersion, the rhetoric of self-deflation or self-martyrdom, the poem merely exhales one more of those innumerable sighs with which the poet nourishes himself in the solipsistic taking back of that which he gives forth. "Il suono / di quei sospiri ond'io nudriva 'l core" is the sound of these words themselves. It is a sound that continues to nourish the poet as he passes a despairing judgment on the past. The rhetoric of temporal referentiality—"those sighs . . . when . . ."—gives way to the performative instance of enunciation. Linear dispersion becomes a circle of lyric containment. That which time disperses—the self's integrity—the poet regathers or reconstitutes in the lyric sonority of lament. Time's discontinuous extensions are brought together and reorganized in the sound and rhythms of the lyric's measured music.

In these sounds the self weeps over its failure to reappropriate itself, even as the reappropriation takes place in the musical resolution of the poem's artifice. Hence the master myth of the Canzoniere: Apollo's pursuit of Daphne. The intangible nymph is transformed into a laurel tree at the moment of her appropriation by the god of music, the way tears and lament turn to music on the stage—the poem—where the self confesses its secret drama. In this sense lament provides the insubstantial substance, or the sighs, that nourish the anthology's poems. So too the insubstantial, rhetorical self constitutes itself anew with each act of poetic enunciation. But as the sighs expire so does the artifice of the lyric self.[20]

Only a poet who had pursued such solipsism to its extreme could have produced the unlikely verse in the third stanza of "Voi ch'ascoltate" which reads: "di me medesmo meco mi vergogno." The multiplication of self-reflexive morphemes encloses this voice within the circle of its own production of the fruit of shame. And what is shame if not an aggravated state of self-reflexivity? This is the shame, or better the mortality, that nourishes and perpetuates the voice of lament. As Petrarch reminds us time and again, it is the lament of Narcissus bound to an image that has no corporeal density, that cannot be rendered substantial, since its otherness figures as a hollow projection of the self's shadow.[21]

6 Beyond the Lyric

The "Donna Gentile"   The *Vita Nuova* is a different kind of anthology than the *Rime sparse*. It is at once more and less than an anthology of poems. The narrative dimension of the work provides a temporal framework in which the ideal present tense of the poems is seen in the light of an absolute past tense. The prose tells a story of how the poems came to be composed in time, thus providing a temporal continuum, or linear extension, which subverts the monadic principle of lyric containment and crystallization. But to tell a story, properly speaking, means more than merely to narrate events in chronological time; it means above all to construct an intrigue and unfold a drama. Dante's prose does precisely that, for the narrative is organized according to a "plot." The protagonist's confrontation with and repudiation of what I have called the Petrarchan alternative constititute a nodal moment in this plot, and it is because of this repudiation that we have a plot instead of a mere chronicle of events. Plot, in its colligation of events, represents a wholly different alternative to the Petrarchan model. Posed in these terms, lyric is not opposed to narrative in any absolute way but is opposed to the kind of narrative which relies on plot as its organizing principle. However persuasively one may argue for a narrative design to Petrarch's anthology, one still faces the absence of narrative intrigue and resolution in the *Canzoniere*.

Paul Ricoeur, who has broken new ground in his recent work on time and narrative, defines plot as "the intelligible whole that governs a succession of events in a story. . . . A story is *made out of* events to the extent that plot *makes* events into a story. The plot, therefore, places us at the crossing point of temporality and narrativity." Now the death of Beatrice is not in itself enough to constitute a plot, for what is necessary for plot is a "predicament that calls for thinking, action, or both. . . . The answer to this predicament advances the story to its conclusion."[1] Seen from the perspective of narrative logic, the death of Beatrice is insufficient to advance the *libello* to its dramatic fulfillment in chapter XLII. A "predicament" is needed, and it is precisely the predicament of the *donna gentile* which, calling for an answer, advances the *Vita Nuova* to its conclusion. While the death of Beatrice remains central to the plot's configuration, the plot actually weaves its intrigue around the episode of the appearance of this woman in the story.

Singleton believed that the death of Beatrice was a sufficient event for the master narrative of the *Vita Nuova*, but as I remarked in the Introduction, he refused to read beyond it. He has almost nothing to say about the *donna gentile* and accounts for the passage from the "second" to the "third" stage of the narrative in terms of Beatrice's death alone. "The effects of love on the lover [first Cavalcantian stage] and the praise of the lady [second stage] belong to the tradition. The death of Beatrice [the third and last stage, representing a transition from contemplative love to Christian *caritas*] does not. As the poet begins to make his copy out of the Book of Memory, Beatrice is already dead and in glory."[2] Here too Singleton rewrites the *Vita Nuova* for us. These "stages" are altogether questionable; in any case there is no doubt that after Beatrice's death Dante returns to the so-called first stage. His encounter with the *donna gentile* disrupts the framework of progression and brings together the various strands of the plot in what amounts to the central crisis of the work: the crisis of literary alternatives. Let us follow the story.

Chapter XXXIV: Beatrice is dead. Dante has composed no poems for almost a year. Privation and mourning: the lyric voice is faltering. On the first anniversary of Beatrice's death,

Dante sits aimlessly remembering her, sketching angel figures on "certe tavolette." A group of men approach him but he is so lost in thought that he does not immediately become aware of their presence. Shortly thereafter the idea for a sonnet comes to him. His first attempt to compose it results in an abortive first stanza, which Dante calls the *primo cominciamento* of the sonnet "Era venuta." In a second attempt, the *secondo cominciamento*, he succeeds in completing the poem. For some reason, however, the author includes in the *Vita Nuova* the abortive *primo cominciamento* of the sonnet. We are forced to wonder why, or for what dramatic purpose, the implosive lines of that first beginning are provided for Dante's reader. What purpose does the inclusion serve? One explanation is that it indicates the poet's faltering, his groping for the lost voice of lyricism; another explanation is that it intends to draw attention to the fact that, for some reason, the articulation of these original lines arrived at an impasse beyond which it could not proceed. Here are the two beginnings:

Primo Cominciamento
Era venuta ne la mente mia
la gentil donna che per suo valore
fu posta da l'altissimo signore
nel ciel de l'umiltate, ov'è Maria.

Secondo Cominciamento
Era venuta ne la mente mia
quella donna gentil cui piange Amore,
entro 'n quel punto che lo suo valore
vi trasse a riguardar quel ch'eo facia.

Amor, che ne la mente la sentia,
s'era svegliato nel destrutto core,
e diceva a' sospiri: "Andate fore";
per che ciascun dolente si partia.

Piangendo uscivan for de lo mio petto
con una voce che sovente mena
le lagrime dogliose a li occhi tristi.

Ma quei che n'uscian for con maggior pena,
venian dicendo: "Oi nobile intelletto,
oggi fa l'anno che nel ciel salisti."

(xxv, 7–11)

First Beginning
There came into my mind
the gentle lady who for her virtue
was placed by our most exalted lord
in the heaven of humility, where Mary is.

Second Beginning
There came into my mind
that gentle lady who is wept by love,
precisely at that moment when her influence [on me]
caused you to observe what I was doing.

Love, who felt her in the mind,
had woken up in the distraught heart,
and was saying to my sighs: "Go out";
and so each one left in grief.

Weeping they exited from my chest
with a voice that often brings
grieving tears to my sorry eyes.

But those that left with the greatest pain
came saying: "O noble intellect,
today makes a year that you rose to heaven."

Even though Cavalcanti drops out of the narrative in chapter xxx, the ghost of the "primo amico" still haunts this poem, as indeed it haunts the entire episode of the *donna gentile*. Its Cavalcantianism is perhaps appropriate to the emotion of disorientation and *sbigottimento* which follows Beatrice's demise, but why does the *primo cominciamento* fail to get beyond itself? We may isolate three motifs in the first stanza of the second beginning, absent from the first, which apparently enabled Dante to finish the poem:

1. The motif of lament. Whereas the first beginning contains no allusion to tears or grievance, the second speaks of a woman "cui piange Amore."

2. The motif of spectators. The second beginning introduces the presence of spectators where before there were no spectators ("*vi* trasse a riguardar quel ch'eo facia"). These spectators are the men who happened upon Dante while he was lost in thought sketching angel figures.

3. The motif of the self. The first beginning bypasses the role of the self and seems to implode as a result. The single stanza gives total priority to the lady glorified in heaven, but that supersphere ("ciel de l'umiltate") is far too remote for a self that still positions itself within the space of the widowed city. In effect, the poet's concern at this point is the absence of which *he* is the measure, not the presence of which Beatrice is the measure. Thus, the second beginning, which introduces a mourning subject ("cui *piange* Amore"; "vi trasse a riguardar quel ch'*eo* facia"), allows the poet to reorient the poem away from the lady and toward the self. Indeed, the rest of the poem speaks exclusively about the state of the mourning self. The "gentle lady" at her remote distance effectively disappears from the poem, while the poet's tears and sorrow take over. The distancing of Beatrice is already signaled in the second beginning by the substitution for the definite article *la* with the demonstrative pronoun *quella* in the second verse.

These three motifs—lament, spectators, and the self—not only allow the *secondo cominciamento* to get under way but also prepare for and circumscribe Dante's encounter with the *donna gentile*. The encounter takes place in the next chapter and involves all three temptations. Dante is once again sitting somewhere remembering the past and grieving: "io fosse in parte ne la quale mi ricordava del passato tempo, molto stava pensoso, e con dolorosi pensamenti, tanto che mi faceano parere de fore una vista di terribile sbigottimento" ["I was in a place that reminded me of past times, buried in thought and with sorrowful ruminations, so much so that it gave my appearance an aspect of terrible distress"]. With mournful melancholia written in his aspect, he raises his eyes and sees himself observed by a young woman standing in a window. The staging of the scene is remarkable:

> Onde io, accorgendomi del mio travagliare, levai li
> occhi per vedere se altri mi vedesse. Allora vidi una
> gentile donna giovane e bella molto, la quale da una
> finestra mi riguardava sì pietosamente, quanto a la
> vista, che tutta la pietà parea in lei accolta. Onde,
> con ciò sia cosa che quando li miseri veggiono di loro
> compassione altrui, più tosto si muovono a
> lagrimare, quasi come di se stessi avendo pietate,
> io sentí allora cominciare li miei occhi a volere
> piangere. (XXXV, 1–4)

> Then, becoming aware of my own distress, I raised
> my eyes to see if anyone else was seeing me. And so
> I saw a gentle lady, young and beautiful, who was
> looking at me from a window so piteously that, to
> judge from the appearance, all pity seemed to be
> gathered within her. And because a miserable person
> is easier moved to tears when he sees compassion
> in others, almost as if taking pity on himself, I felt
> my eyes begin to want to cry.

The passage describes a visual specularity whereby the self returns to itself through the image of the other in a reflective medium, in this case a window. Here then is a spectator. Dante has been looking for one. We notice that even before he saw the woman, he raised his eyes to see if he was being seen, "per vedere se altri mi vedesse." This reflexivity of sight sums up the specularity that will characterize the encounter with the new woman. Her visible compassion comes from the visible signs of grief Dante wears on his face, so much so that her eyes become a visionary monitor of his inward distress.[3]

Dante begins to fall in love with this lady because she has

"una vista pietosa e d'un colore pallido quasi come d'amore" ["a face of mercy and of a pale color almost like love's"]. It seems as if she will substitute for Beatrice by virtue of a similitude: "Onde molte fiate mi ricordava de la mia nobilissima donna, che di simile colore si mostrava tuttavia" ["Wherefore many times she reminded me of my noble lady, for she showed herself in similar colors"]. Yet the woman's likeness to Beatrice is wholly insubstantial. While the corporeal opacity of Beatrice gave density to her otherness, the *donna gentile* is pure reflection, framed in a window as in a mirror, stripped of otherness. Full of compassion, her face assumes an aspect of grief which literally doubles Dante's own grieving aspect.

Beatrice, on the other hand, denies Dante her greeting.[4]

It is no accident that Dante's new encounter is marked by a *psychomachia* that critics have seen as a relapse into Cavalcantianism. More than Cavalcantianism, however, the inner contradictions, partitions, and divisions that turn the self into a "battlefield," to use Dante's metaphor, seem like a prefiguration of the Petrarchan drama of a self torn between the alternatives of self-love and conversion, between secular desire and spirituality (Dante speaks of the inner battle in terms of heart and soul: "L'una parte chiamo cuore, cioè l'appetito; l'altra chiamo anima, cioè la ragione" [XXXVII, 6]). What remains the same in either case is the fact that the poetic voice is nourished by the strife of the self, not by the inspiration of otherness, and thus becomes a voice of the shadows. For one of the great temptations of the *donna gentile* lies in the power of her reflection to open the ocular channel for Dante's tears and to bring forth poems from him. The link between eyes, tears, and poetry is crucial to the entire episode and to the Petrarchan temptation it represents. For the past year since Beatrice's death the lyric voice has groped in the void of her absence, reduced practically to silence. The *donna gentile* tempts by the power she has to liberate, through reflexive self-pity, the resources of lyric lament and self-preoccupation, in other words, of mourning. Just as she liberates tears from the eyes, so too she calls forth poems from the deprived self. Dante compulsively returns to look at this woman whose compassionate counterlook brings forth both tears and poems from him: "And certainly it happened that many times, being unable to cry and unburden my sadness, I would go to see this woman of pity, who seemed to draw tears forth from my eyes by her sight [*per la sua vista*]. And thus the urge to speak words would come to me" (xxxvi, 2–3). Tears and poems flow together in the work of mourning.[5]

In the absence of Beatrice, who gave life to the voice, Dante finds in the *donna gentile* not a reflection of the other but rather a reflection of the self that has lost the other. The several poems inspired by this "new love" attest to the self's obsession with its mournful subjectivity, and after the fourth sonnet composed for the woman, our poet seems irresistibly drawn to the Petrarchan alternative of specular self-presence, lyric indulgence, and solipsistic narcissism. The knot of the story's intrigue has been tied. The rest of the narrative will undo it.

The Pilgrims   The transcendent disposition unto Beatrice gives way to a solipsistic reflexivity once her death deprives Florence of her presence. The laudatory poem in turn gives way to a narcissistic lyricism, in the deeper Petrarchan sense that we gave to that term. The *donna gentile* tempts by virtue of the specular transparency that keeps the lyric confined to a circle not of incorporation but of mournful subjectivity. We must now follow closely the last chapters of Dante's text if we are to understand how the *Vita Nuova* culminates with an overcoming of lyric stasis and a seizure of narrative dynamism. The end of the work raises broad theoretical questions about the essence of narrative, but before we can address those questions we must follow the events that lead to the last chapter, for on the basis of the logic that underlies these events the end of the work reveals itself as a coherent outcome of all that precedes it.

Chapter xxxix: the *donna gentile* seems on the verge of supplanting Beatrice in Dante's affections, but in one sudden and

unexpected moment, the "malicious desire and vain temptation" of the new love is vaporized:

> Contra questo avversario de la ragione si levoe un
> die, quasi ne l'ora de la nona, una forte imaginazione
> in me, che mi parve vedere questa gloriosa Beatrice
> con quelle vestimenta sanguigne co le quali apparve
> prima a li occhi miei; e pareami giovane in simile
> etade in quale io prima la vidi. Allora cominciai a
> pensare di lei; e ricordandomi di lei secondo l'ordine
> del tempo passato, lo mio cuore cominciò a pentere
> de lo desiderio a cui sì vilmente s'avea lasciato pos-
> sedere alquanti die contra la costanzia de la ragione:
> e discacciato questo cotale malvagio desiderio, sì si
> rivolsero tutti li miei pensamenti a la loro gentilis-
> sima Beatrice. (XXXIX, 1–2)

> Against this adversary of reason there rose up one
> day, almost at nine o'clock, a powerful imagination
> within me, and I seemed to see this glorious Beatrice
> dressed in those crimson garments in which she first
> appeared to my eyes; and she seemed the same young
> age as when I first saw her. And so I began thinking
> about her; and recalling her according to the order
> of time past, my heart began to repent grievously of
> the desire by which it had so vilely allowed itself
> to be possessed for some days against the constancy
> of reason: and having chased this malicious desire
> away, all my thoughts reverted themselves to their
> most gentle Beatrice.

On the surface the passage is about the return of Beatrice's
image in memory. More essentially, however, it is about time's
thematic continuity in Beatrice. We have strong intimations of
restoration: Beatrice reappears in memory dressed in the same
crimson vestments in which she first appeared to Dante's eyes.
An original image is retrieved and "constancy" restored. The
return of her image in memory is accompanied by an emotion

of repentance on Dante's part—an emotion or motion of reflexive relation to the past. While repentance is also a form of *psychomachia*, it is generated by the triumph of the past as opposed to its denial. Along with this repentance comes a repudiation of the *donna gentile*, and all of Dante's thoughts "revert" to Beatrice in an affirmation of the *order* of time: "E ricordandomi di lei secondo *l'ordine* del tempo passato."

The repudiation of the *donna gentile* does not mean, however, a repudiation of the Petrarchan alternative. On the contrary, Petrarch's devotion to Laura was prodigiously constant well after her death. In fact, after rejecting his new love, Dante immediately relapses into the stasis of lament and narcissistic mourning which chararacterized his state just before his encounter with the *donna gentile*. This is clear from the following chapter of the *libello*, which describes Dante's experience with a group of "pilgrims" passing through Florence. The pilgrims are journeying to Rome to see the veil of Veronica, "quella imagine benedetta la quale Iesu Cristo lasciò a noi per essemplo de la sua bellissima figura" (XL, I) ["that blessed image which Jesus Christ left us as an exemplum of his beautiful face"]. Dante calls the wayfarers *pilgrims* "in the broad sense" ("secondo la larga significazione"), to mean people who find themselves outside their own country. *Pilgrim* in the narrower sense, he says, means someone who makes his or her way to the sanctuary of St. James in Galicia. Those people who travel in devotion to God fall under three specific rubrics: the "palmieri" travel across the sea to the Holy Land, where they gather palms; the "peregrini," or pilgrims, travel to St. James's sanctuary; and the "romei," or "Romers," are the people who travel to Rome to see the veil of Veronica.

The motif of pilgrimage brings to mind the *Commedia*'s protagonist, who journeys through the afterworld like a "pilgrim," though whether in the broad or the narrow sense is far from clear. Pilgrimage figures as a dynamic, teleological movement across an alien expanse, and whatever else it may represent in the *Commedia*, such as moral or spiritual journey, it represents first and foremost the fact of narrative itself: the progressive development of a story toward an outcome that follows from the events that lead up to it and from the perspective of which those events constitute a coherent or plausible totality. To the extent that pilgrimage means progressive movement toward a specific destination, it figures as a master emblem of narrative logic itself, which depends wholly upon the role of endings.[6] Clearly the narrative of the *Vita Nuova* relies upon the same essential logic as the epic *Commedia*, whose story moves progressively, like a journey, toward a determinate outcome. Only, in the case of the *libello*, the outcome does not bring closure to the story but rather opens it up to the narrative dynamism that underlies the thematic configuration, with its protagonists, events, setting, "plot," and so forth. How does this opening come about?

The poet or protagonist who sees the pilgrims passing through Florence in chapter XL has no sense of such openness yet, for even at this late stage in the story Dante is still lyrically naive about narrative trajectories and teleologies. He has no sense of an extended horizon, or dynamic *distance*. Or better, the intimate distance of a veil that held him off from Beatrice's naked presence in the marvelous vision has still not been disclosed in its cosmic dimensions.

The text is unambiguous on this point. The pilgrims seem to Dante "from a far-off place," not from a "near town" [*propinquo paese*]. Thinking about these wayfarers, he says to himself:

> "Se io li potesse tenere alquanto, io li pur farei piangere anzi ch'elli uscissero di questa cittade, però che io direi parole le quali farebbero piangere chiunque le intendesse." (XL, 4)

> "If I could stall them for a while, I could surely make them weep before they leave this city, for I would speak words that would make anyone weep."

This private thought reflects the protagonist's continuing lyric and existential stasis (henceforth the literary disposition becomes inseparable from an existential disposition, and Dante's attainment of a new literary alternative will come as the consequence of an existential *prise de conscience*). He would like to *arrest* the journey of the pilgrims. In the sonnet he composes on this occasion, he deploys images of movement and spatial extension only in order to make a plea for arrestation and stasis:

> Deh peregrini che pensosi andate,
> forse di cosa che non v'è presente,
> venite voi da sì lontana gente,
> com'a la vista voi ne dimostrate,
>
> che non piangete quando vol passate
> per lo suo mezzo la città dolente,
> come quelle persone che neente
> par che 'ntendesser la sua gravitate?
>
> Se voi restate per volerlo audire,
> certo lo cor de' sospiri mi dice
> che lagrimando n'uscirete pui.
>
> Ella ha perduta la sua beatrice
> e le parole ch'om di lei pò dire
> hanno vertù di far piangere altrui.
>
> (XL, 9–10)

> O you pilgrims who move pensively along,
> thinking perhaps of something that is not present here,
> do you come from such a far-off place,
> as you show from your faces,
>
> that you don't even weep when you pass
> through the middle of the grieving city,
> like people who seem to know nothing
> about the grave sorrows afflicting it?
>
> If you stay awhile to hear about it,
> my sighing heart tells me that certainly you
> will not leave this place without weeping.

She has lost her beatrice;
and the words that a man can say about her
have the power to make others weep.

The sixth verse—"through the middle of the grieving city"—marks the center of Dante's troubled lyric topology: a space of lament, negative presence, and stasis. The rhyme words *dolente* and *neente* gravitate around this center like phonetic and semantic descents into the "gravitate" of the grieving city. We need not stress that the transcendent movement of these pilgrims through and beyond the city of Florence repeats or reenacts Beatrice's movement into and out of the lyric topology. Beatrice literally came and went. In Dante's sonnet, however, lyric stasis and narrative dynamism come together in the mode of conflict. The conflict is one of extension versus closure, loss versus recuperation, perhaps even Florence versus Rome; but above all it is a conflict between active transit and sedentary passivity.[7]

Perhaps this is the place to remark how the *Vita Nuova* consistently portrays its protagonist as a passive subject who waits for things to *come* to him, to *occur* to him, to *reach* him. The notion of passivity pervades the narrative in descriptive phrases like: "mi *giunse* uno pensamento forte" ["a strong thought reached me"]; "pensando a lei mi *sopragiunse* uno soave sonno" ["thinking of her I was overcome by a soft sleep"]; "in questa imaginazione mi *giunse* tanta umiltade di vedere lei" ["in this fantasy there came to me such humility to see her"]; "in alcuna parte de la mia persona mi *giunse* una dolorosa infermitade" ["a painful illness attained a certain part of my person"]; "*vennemi* volontade di volere dire" ["the will to say something came to me"]; "mi *mosse* una volontade di dire parole" ["I was moved by a desire to speak"]. Consider also the protagonist's sedentary disposition in those several instances when he happens to be seated, doing nothing, and something happens, or when he is induced into activity because of the initiative of someone else: "sedendo io in alcuna parte" ["being seated somewhere"]; "io mi sedea in parte" ["I was seated in a place"]; "alcuno amico mi venisse a dire" ["a friend came to tell me"]; "io fui condotto per amica persona" ["I was led there by a friend of mine"]. If one were to catalogue the instances of subjective passivity signaled by the narrative, one would have to include the numerous occurrences of the verb *apparire* coupled with a reflexive pronoun, indicating a passive subject of perception: "m'apparve" and "apparve a me."[8]

The passivity of the lyric disposition, however, is also the necessary condition for its inspiration. But with Beatrice's disappearance from the local topology of the lyric, the fullness of aesthetic stasis that graced "Tanto gentile" gives way to the privations of existential stasis expressed in Dante's first sonnet to the pilgrims. Nonetheless, Dante's experience with the pilgrims does something to rouse him from this sedentary disposition. It somehow brings about a new awareness of extension, distance, and cosmological space. Dante calls this new awareness an "intelligenza nova." Its advent is signaled by the last poem of the *Vita Nuova*, "Oltre la spera," which describes the cosmic ascent of Dante's sigh beyond the widest sphere of the heavens, high above the local confines of Florence. Before reading the sonnet let us see what transpires between the penultimate poem of the *Vita Nuova*, which we have just read, and this ultimate poem, which shows that the spell of lyric elegy is about to be broken.

The opening of chapter XLI, which follows immediately after the sonnet "Deh peregrini," offers us subtle clues about what leads to the breakthrough:

> Poi [i peregrini] mandarono due donne gentili a me pregando che io mandasse loro queste mie parole rimate; onde io, pensando la loro nobiltade, propuosi di mandare loro e di fare una cosa nuova, la quale io mandasse a loro con esse, acciò che più onorevolement adempiesse li loro prieghi. E dissi allora uno sonetto, lo quale narra del mio stato, e manda' lo a loro co lo precedente sonetto accompagnato. . . (XLI, 1–3)

> Then they [the pilgrims] sent two gentle ladies to me
> to ask that I send them these verses of mine; so I,
> thinking of their nobility, decided to send them and to
> compose something new, which I would send along
> with these ladies, so as to fulfill their request more
> honorably. And so I wrote a sonnet in which I nar-
> rated my state, and I sent it to them accompanied with
> the preceding sonnet. . . .

From the perspective of biographical realism, the idea that these anonymous pilgrims would send "two gentle ladies" to Florence to request that Dante send them his poem lacks plausibility. From the perspective of narrative logic, however, the staging of the episode is crucial. The verb *mandare*, "to send," occurs five times in this short passage. The poem "Oltre la spera"—which Dante refers to as the "cosa nuova" here—seems to originate with Dante's awareness that the poem will be sent to the pilgrims at a distant location. It would seem that the poem's destiny of being sent abroad in the hands of two ladies discloses for Dante the cosmic space of pilgrimage which his sigh will traverse in the poem itself. The poem's telegenesis, its distant destination that it takes up metaphorically in its own poetic figurations, liberates what amounts to a new horizon of referentiality:

> Oltre la spera che più larga gira
> passa 'l sospiro ch'esce del mio core:
> intelligenza nova, che l'Amore
> piangendo mette in lui, pur su lo tira.
>
> Quand'elli è giunto là dove disira,
> vede una donna, che riceve onore,
> e luce sì, che per lo suo splendore
> lo peregrino spirito la mira.
>
> Vedela tal, che quando 'l mi ridice,
> io no lo intendo, sì parla sottile
> al cor dolente, che lo fa parlare.

So che parla di quella gentile,
però che spesso ricorda Beatrice,
sì ch'io lo 'ntendo ben, donne mie care.

(XLI, 10–13)

Beyond the sphere that most widely turns
passes the sigh that exits from my heart:
a new intelligence, which lamentful love
gives to it, draws it upward.

When it has reached the place that it desires,
it sees a woman who receives honor
and who shines, such that through her splendor
the pilgrim spirit can look on her.

But when it tells me in what guise it has seen her,
I cannot understand it, so subtle is its speech
to the grieving heart that makes it speak.

I know that it speaks about that gentle one,
since it often reminds me of Beatrice,
so that I understand it well, my dear ladies.

The destinations of pilgrimage splinter into a multiplicity. The pilgrims passing through Florence head toward the veil of Veronica, which bears the "true imprint" of Christ's face. The material poem we have just read travels like a pilgrim outside of Florence to reach the pilgrims to whom it is addressed. The sigh in Dante's poem, on the other hand, undertakes a pilgrimage to behold Beatrice in her place of destination. The great lyric sigh of "Tanto gentile" has now become a "pilgrim spirit" rising beyond the widest sphere to retrieve a vision of Beatrice in her place of destination, after she, too, like an existential pilgrim, passed through Florence during her temporal life.

In a rigorous study of the medieval fusions and confusions of older esoteric traditions, Robert Klein has shown the extent to which the *Vita Nuova* engages Neoplatonic theories of the pneumatological return of the spirit to its place of belonging.[9] The pilgrim spirit's journey beyond the widest sphere toward the place where motion comes to repose appears to tell a Platonic story of the erotic or pneumatological return of the soul to its own proper domicile. But we must be careful here, for Dante's specific notion of pilgrimage revises the story of a Platonic flight of the soul. Dante calls his sigh a pilgrim spirit "acciò che spiritualmente va là suso, e sì come peregrino lo quale è fuori de la sua patria, vi stae" ["because it goes up spiritually, and remains there as a pilgrim who is outside of his country"]. The ascent of the sigh is *not* a return to the place of origin but rather an expatriation. Insofar as the spirit belongs with the poet's heart, whence it departed, the real return of this spirit is its elliptical descent back to earth, to Florence, and to the poet's heart.

The second part of Dante's sonnet deals in fact with the spirit's return to its own proper domicile. There it speaks about what it has seen up above, but Dante cannot understand its "subtle speech," for the noumenal vision of Beatrice which informs it makes its speech unintelligible. Yet Dante knows that it speaks of Beatrice because the spirit returns to him with an authentic imprint of Beatrice on its speech : "almeno intendo questo, cioè che tutto è lo cotale pensare de la mia donna, però ch'io sento lo suo nome spesso nel mio pensero" ["this much at least I understand, that it is all a thinking about my lady, for I often hear her name in my thought"]. The name of Beatrice verifies the spirit's speech about her, and although Dante cannot understand the speech, he understands that it talks of Beatrice because her proper name pervades it. But once again, the veiled quality of the speech derives from the fact that the sigh's journey authenticates its language as a true representation, or image, of its transcendent vision. The spirit's speech is precisely that: a veil with a true imprint of Beatrice's image on it. In other words, a Veronica.[10]

Veils of Representation Given the conspicuous intersections between "Oltre la spera" and the occasion that produced it, given also the Christological terms in which Dante represents Beatrice in the *Vita Nuova*, and given, finally, that the pilgrim sigh in "Oltre la spera" journeys toward Beatrice and returns to earth with her image imprinted upon its unintelligible speech, the veil of Veronica evoked in XL must be seen as a figure for an authentic language of representation with regard to Beatrice.

The *Vita Nuova* is in the final analysis a story about the trials and errors, the false starts and breakthroughs, in a poet's attempt to find a language adequate to this woman. The work ends with the author's hypothesis of a wholly new, more worthy language than he has had at his disposal until this point. It ends, in other words, with the author resolving upon a literary destination, a destination like that which oriented the pilgrims journeying toward the Veronica in Rome. This is the veil that bears the true image of Christ's face, "quella imagine benedetta la quale Iesu Cristo lasciò a noi per essemplo de la sua bellissima figura, la quale vede la mia donna gloriosamente" ["that blessed image which Jesus Christ left us as an exemplum of his beautiful face, which my lady gloriously beholds"]. In the complex pattern of analogy which dominates the text here, the difference between seeing the face itself and seeing its image on the veil amounts to the difference between the pilgrim spirit's noumenal vision of Beatrice in heaven and its "subtle speech" upon its return, the speech that speaks to Dante of what it has seen. To come into the strange, authenticated language of this veiled speech will be the destination Dante sets for himself at the close of the work.

The motifs of veil, image, figure, and representation lead us back to the genetic source of these authenticated phenomenalities, namely, the body of Beatrice. What makes the Veronica an authentic representation or "true icon," as the etymon would suggest, is the fact that it received its imprint from the body of Christ. The object of its representation is the genesis of the rep-

resentation. In terms of the *Vita Nuova*'s story of the genesis of a
literary career, representation here means poetic speech not
only "about" Beatrice but above all generated by Beatrice.

Meanwhile it seems as if the crimson veil wrapped around
the body of Beatrice in Dante's marvelous vision has been left
behind. In truth the veil of Veronica is merely a transfigured
version of this crimson veil, which in turn is the originary figure
of Beatrice's phenomenality. Just as the noumenal body that
underlay the veil authenticated her phenomenality, so too it
authenticated, as long as Beatrice lived, the ideal lyrics that in-
corporated her presence into their felicitous praise. With the
absence of Beatrice, however, appearances become empty and
simulacrous and lyric speech loses access to the source of its new
life. The death of Beatrice gives the crimson cloth an entirely
new determination; it is no longer the veil that conceals the
body and re-presents its presence in and through the veil itself,
for it is now a veil of the future. One makes one's way toward it.
It now marks the distance that holds Dante off from a new language.

But what are the terms of this future and in what manner
are they disclosed to Dante? How does it happen that the distensions of time open themselves up in such a way that Dante
can take leave of the lyric province of Florence and move toward an epic goal—toward "Rome," so to speak? The pilgrim
spirit in "Oltre la spera" returns to the lyric topology of Florence with an unintelligible speech that leaves Dante disori-
ented, turning that topology into a region of unlikeness. How,
then, does the new life become possible as the story we have
followed up until this point?

7 The Narrative Breakthrough

Appresso questo sonetto apparve a me una mirabile visione, ne la quale io vidi cose che mi fecero proporre di non dire più di questa benedetta infino a tanto che io potesse più degnamente trattare di lei. E di venire a ciò io studio quanto posso, sì com'ella sae veracemente. Sì che, se piacere sarà di colui a cui tutte le cose vivono, che la mia vita duri per alquanti anni, io spero di dicer di lei quello che mai non fue detto d'alcuna. E poi piaccia a colui che è sire de la cortesia, che la mia anima se ne possa gire a vedere la gloria de la sua donna, cioè di quella benedetta Beatrice, la quale gloriosamente mira ne la faccia di colui *qui est per omnia secula benedictus*. (XLII, 1–3)

Soon after this sonnet there appeared to me a miraculous vision, in which I saw things that made me resolve to say no more about this blesséd one until I could speak of her more worthily. And to arrive at this [goal] I am studying as much as I can, as she truly knows. And if it will be the pleasure of him to whom all things live that my life last a few more years, I hope to say of her that which has never been said of any woman. And then may it please him who is the lord of courtesy that my soul may go to see the glory of its woman, that is, that blesséd Beatrice, who gloriously gazes into the face of he *qui est per omnia secula benedictus*.

This is the ending that has enchanted, baffled, and divided readers of the *Vita Nuova* over the centuries. It enchants by its naive anticipation of the *Commedia* presumably years before Dante had conceived the poem. It baffles by its declaration that the *libello* we have just finished reading fails to treat its matter adequately and that the real book remains to be written sometime in the future. Finally, it divides those who uphold its originality from those who, for various reasons, believe that Dante revised the original ending of the work much later in his career. Amid the enigmas surrounding the chapter—and they are many—this much at least seems clear, that such an ending qualifies the *Vita Nuova* as the first of Dante's unfinished works. The *libello* comes to an end, but the author projects its story beyond the bounds of the narrative.

Unfinished does not mean unterminated, however. Unlike the subsequent *De vulgari eloquentia* and *Convivio*, the *Vita Nuova* arrives at a terminal conclusion from the perspective of which the work reveals itself as a totality and not as a fragment. Open-endedness becomes a principle of necessity, an operative logic, an essential element of the work's wholeness rather than the result of fragmentation. The promise to continue, the projection of a task for the future, the author's avowal of his failure not only to have accomplished but even to have apprehended his literary vocation until this point—these dynamics of the last chapter terminate the narrative but at the same time recapitulate the logic that sustained it from the beginning. What I shall try to demonstrate in this chapter is how the *libello* ends with a momentous vision of temporal extension that provides the horizon for the narrative dynamism of the *Vita Nuova* and allows for the projection of its story beyond the bounds of the last chapter.

In his recent work on narrative, which is of particular interest to us here, Paul Ricoeur formulates the relation between time and narrative in the following terms:

> [A] narrated story, governed in its totality by its way
> of ending, constitutes an alternative to the represen-

tation of time as flowing from past to future, according to the well known metaphor of the "arrow of time." It is as if recollection would invert the so-called "natural" order of time. By reading the end in the beginning and the beginning in the end, we learn also how to read time itself against the grain, as the recapitulation of the initial conditions of a course of action in its terminal consequences.[1]

Ricoeur also notes that what defines the beginning of a narrative is not the "absence of antecedence" but an "absence of necessity in the succession." Likewise, an end is not merely that which "comes after" something else, but that which comes, as Aristotle says, "either by virtue of necessity or of probability" (*Poetics*, 50b 30). By this "reduction to form,"[2] the end of a story reveals the intelligible logic that brought its events to that point. This revelation, in its recapitulative character, *is* in some sense the end.

The *Vita Nuova* conforms to this logic of narrative ends and at the same time escapes it. There exists what one could call a logic of transcendence in the story, a logic that, from the beginning, sustains the protagonist's movement from one threshold of experience to another in his conversion to Beatrice. Indeed, what we call the story's "action" is essentially the sum of impasses and breakthroughs which articulate it: the case of the screen ladies, Beatrice's denial of her greeting, the poem of praise, the death of Beatrice, the *donna gentile*'s "vain temptation," and so on. By the end of the *libello*, the interruption or suspension that brings it to a close has become for the reader a familiar pattern, for once again we find the poet at a threshold of silence in his quest for an adequate idiom with regards to Beatrice. It is by no means the first such threshold. We need only recall the protagonist's vow of silence earlier in the narrative, when he comes to realize that a certain poetic manner has been inadequate and that a new one is somehow necessary. In chapter XVII, one of the shortest of the *Vita Nuova*, the poet

suspends his enterprise in a manner that is strikingly similar to
what occurs at the end of the work:

> Poi che dissi questi tre sonetti . . . credendomi tacere e
> non dire più . . . avvegna che sempre poi tacesse di
> dire a lei, a me covenne ripigliare matera nuova e più
> nobile che la passata. (XVII, 1)

> After I had written these three sonnets . . . believing
> I should remain silent and say no more . . . I spoke no
> more to her, and it behooved me to find a new and
> more noble theme than the past one.

Dante's decision in XVII to remain silent and to seek out a
more "noble theme" marks one of the turning points of the
story, preparing the way for his discovery of the new hyperspace of lyric praise. But at the end of the *libello*, where once
again the poet feels the need for "matera nuova e più nobile che
la passata," the suspension leaves Dante not only at a literary
threshold but also at an existential one. This is the differential
trait of the last chapter. The convergence of the literary and
existential dimensions of the protagonist's experience reveals
what is at stake for Dante in literary alternatives. This same
convergence requires of us a reorientation of our critical focus
as well as our terminology, for we must now attempt to understand how the narrative breakthrough is linked to a fundamental revolution in Dante's experience of time.

The awakening occasioned by the miraculous vision forces
a crisis of revision on the totality of the poetic project. It signals
the advent of what I am tempted to call a Christian "existential-
ity," with its particular narrative configuration of human and
historical time. It is on the basis of a particular existential temporality that the narrative recapitulation of the new life, which
we as readers have just followed to its conclusion, becomes possible. How so?

The threshold at the end of the *Vita Nuova* is not merely a
literary one, with the author groping once again for an ade-

quate style of representation. Whatever the literary impasse at which the author arrives here, it comes about because of a new vision of the magnitude of existential time, that is to say, the linear extension of human existence, as opposed to the cyclicality of seasons or the stable presence of eternity. Even a superficial grammatical review of the last chapter shows that past, present, and future come together in a dense verbal mass whose various tenses and moods divide, dispose, and coordinate the temporal configuration. Narrative time, in other words, becomes possible for the first time with the new organization reflected in the verbs. A breakdown of the twenty-four verbs that occur in the chapter will help us see exactly what sort of threshold Dante arrives at here, at the end of his narrative. A review of table 1 should be followed by a rereading of the chapter.

The temporal distensions contained in this cluster of verbs receive their disposition and coordination on the basis of the *present tense of narrative time* ("io studio," "io spero," etc.). This narrative present tense (which is wholly different in nature than Petrarch's ideal lyric present tense) divides the has-been from the not-yet and becomes the dynamic measure, in a certain sense, of what is past and what is still to come. It is a

TABLE I Verbs Occurring in Chapter XLII of the *Vita Nuova*

	Indicative		Subjunctive	Infinitive
Past	*Present*	*Future*		
apparve	studio	sarà	potesse	proporre
vidi	posso		duri	dire
fecero	sae		piaccia	trattare
fue detto	spero		possa	venire
	mira			dicer
	vivono			gire
	è			vedere
	est			

present tense that refers to a moment in time with a history and a future, a moment that will perforce be superceded in the narrative projection that contains it. In other words, it is not an ideal but a "real" present tense. In Petrarch's case, time's ecstasies were measured by the ideal present tense of the speaking voice—ideal because in its obsessive repetition it refused to enter a diachronic horizon. Here, in the last chapter of the *libello*, however, the present tense of the narrative voice situates itself fully within the dynamism of a progressive temporality. I have said that it acts as the dynamic measure of time's extensions, and while this is true it is only part of the "story." We must now see how the narrative present receives *its* measure from some other, adventitious dimension independent of existential time. Thanks to the intervention of this dimension the totality of narrative time receives a decisive order. Let us examine the text more closely.

Alongside the narrative present, there is also a nontemporal present tense in some of the verbs. These are verbs that refer to a different order of time altogether. In fact, only half of the verbs in the present indicative refer to secular time, that is to say to the chronology associated with the narrative present: "io studio," "[io] posso," "io spero," and "tutte le cose vivono." The other four verbs in the present indicative refer to the order of divine and eternal presence: "[Beatrice] sae"; "[Dio] è"; "[Beatrice] mira"; "[*Deus*] *est*." The two orders of time indicated by the same present tense constitute two separate ontological domains: the chronological now of human finitude, with its past and future dimensions, and God's eternal now, which lies beyond the widest sphere. This latter is the now of totalized time which gathers all past and future into the eternal presence of God's *est*.

What brings the *Vita Nuova* to an end is the conjunction of these two orders of time. The conjuction, in turn, marks the beginning of the new life.[3]

We are not told what Dante saw in the "miraculous vision" but we know that it entailed a vision of Beatrice's own visionary beatitude. The vision was "miraculous" to the extent that *vision marks the mode of Beatrice's beatitude*: "quella benedetta Beatrice, la quale gloriosamente *mira* ne la faccia di colui *qui est per omnia secula benedictus.*" What Beatrice sees gloriously (i.e., eternally) is the eternal presence, the divine *est*, which gathers the totality of time within itself and disposes its secular order. Dante's *mira*culous vision is that of Beatrice's beatitude as she looks (*mira*) into the face of he who sees all things immediately in their presence through divine *theoria*: a direct, totalized, and atemporal "seeing" of all things in their relative being. God relates and keeps in his immediate view all temporal things that exist through and toward him ("a cui tutte le cose vivono"), and beatitude consists essentially in the aesthetic fullness, the aesthetic stasis, of such cosmic speculation.

The miraculous vision marks a radically new beginning from the perspective of which existential time receives an integration with the projected end of all temporal things, that is to say, God. Existential time now takes its measure not from the ideal present tense of the speaking voice but from the absolute present tense of those verbs that refer to the eternal *est*. In other words, the new life receives from this vision a narrative structure that grants closure to the temporal sequence. In a reflection that bears deep correlations with our interrogation, Ricoeur remarks that it is impossible to write a narrative of the historical present, for it could only be an anticipation of how the present will appear to, or what it will mean for, the future (*Temps et récit*, pp. 208–9). The author of the *Vita Nuova* can no more write the story of his personal present than a historian of his historical present. In order for the new life to assume its character as a story, the present tense of narrative time becomes wholly subordinated, in XLII, to an eternal present tense, thanks to which Dante can now project his life into the existential future and, through this projection, anticipate an end point of temporal containment. As such, the new life is projected along a linear, teleological axis that grants it direction as well as a determinate, if deferred, closure. This closure is nothing less than a *second* vision that hypothetically will redeem the trajectory and make existential time "meaningful" by virtue of its directionality.

Figure 1 serves to illustrate the narrative containment of existential time in between two poles of transcendent vision. The new life turns into a cosmic story. Progressing along the horizontal axis, it begins with the miraculous vision, continues in the present with the author's resolve to remain silent, and extends into a future in which he hopes to write of Beatrice what has never been written of any woman. It ends hypothetically with a second vision of Beatrice in her glory, thus closing the circle, or triangle, between one visionary moment and another. In both cases it is Beatrice's own vision that represents the "content" of vision. Meanwhile, between these two moments, the horizontal axis of existential time becomes radically linear.

Linearity belongs only to existential time, however. The fact that the horizontal line comes to an end, where it is conjoined with another order of time, means that the totality of the new life is both "episodic" and "configurational," to adopt the terms that Louis O. Mink uses to speak of narrative structures, that is to say, structures that allow episodic or discrete events to be "grasped together" as an intelligible whole.[4] Stories constitute precisely such intelligible wholes as they subordinate the episodic to the configurational dimension. Thus, not only is Dante's new life *told* as a story, it actually *is* a story to the degree that he envisions the conjunction of the episodic dimension (on the horizontal axis of existential time) with the configurational dimension, namely the episodic dimension's containment within the limits of a progression toward a second vision of Beatrice.

Dante's story of course has a highly specific configuration that derives from, or participates in, the master narrative of Christianity. The new life turns into an analogue, as it were, of salvation history. Salvation history is that grand narrative, perhaps even an epitomy of narrative, which puts the totality of

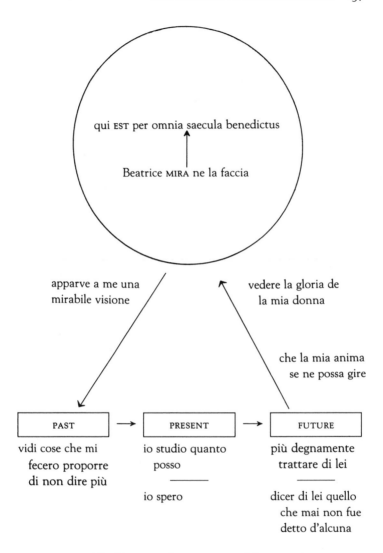

FIGURE I   The Narrative Containment of Existential Time

historical time after the Incarnation on a linear trajectory stretching between the first and second comings. God's intervention in secular time brings about the fusion of divorced ontological orders and thereby gives historical time its narrative (and narratable) order. History becomes the narrative of redemption; redemption becomes the narrative of history; and narrative in the grand sense becomes the *meaning* of secular time as it proceeds along the linear path toward the fulfillment of time in the second coming. As the fulfillment of the first, the second coming marks the plenitude of time, that is to say, the end of the story of all stories and histories.

By an analogy that arises from the essence of Christian schemes of salvation history, existential time in the last chapter of the *Vita Nuova* enters upon a trajectory stretching from one event of divine vision to its fulfilled repetition at the end of that trajectory. Dante's second vision will come about only after he fulfills, in secular time, the event of the first one. The second vision remains in every respect hypothetical, but, once again, it is precisely the hypothetical projection of the end—apocalypse, as it is called in Christianity—that allows for the conjunction of divorced ontological orders and, by extension, for the narrative structure of the new life.

We begin to see how poetics—or better, literary alternatives—are deeply related to this revision in Dante's experience of the horizon of time. To fulfill the event of the miraculous vision means to say of Beatrice what has never been said of any woman. Personal *salvation*, to use a word that recalls the peculiar power of Beatrice's greeting, lies in the seizure of a new manner of representation that is not only adequate to Beatrice but also authenticated by her. Beatrice now means the otherness of the poet's own futurity. We have seen the degree to which Dante links the authentic "veil" of representation to the theme of pilgrimage, and how pilgrimage is in turn linked to the dynamism of the Christian narrative scheme; we have also seen that, while the lyric poem was adequate to the epiphanic phenomenality of Beatrice, it fell into crisis after her death. What then is this new, hypothetical language that would transcend the static cloister of the lyric? How far in the future does it lie and to what extent does its futurity define it?

To call it hypothetical already describes the essence of the language Dante envisions at the close of the *libello*. "Hypothetical" does not mean that he merely projects this language as an eventual possibility for the future; nor does it mean that the lyric of presence merely gives way to prophecy (though prophetic vision is one form the hypothetical may assume); it means rather that projectionality belongs to the fundamental character of this new manner of representation. Just as eschatology allows the totality of secular time to reveal a determinate pattern, so Dante's existential projection toward a terminal future of integration with divine presence imparts to his past life a sense, a new order or meaning, which points forward. The new life in this sense recovers the past and renews it, so to speak. This past had no determinate "sense," or direction, prior to the projection that ends the *libello*, but thanks to this projection the past now becomes recuperable as a story. And what is a story if not a highly determined, temporal configuration of meaning? To express it otherwise, we could say that only because the *libello* ends with a projection into a temporal future can Dante, in his proem, present it as a selective transcription from the "book of memory." The author's narration is not just a narration of past events, is not, that is, a mere chronicle of events, but is, rather, a disclosure of the *meaning* of those events:

> In quella parte del libro de la mia memoria dinanzi a la quale poco si potrebbe leggere, si trova una rubrica la quale dice: *Incipit vita nova*. Sotto la quale rubrica io trovo scritte le parole le quali è mio intendimento d'assemplare in questo libello; e se non tutte, almeno la loro sentenzia. (i, 1–2)

> In that part of the book of my memory before which
> there is little to read, one finds a rubric which says:
> *Incipit vita nova*. Under this rubric I find written
> words that it is my intention to transcribe in this
> little book; and if not all of them then at least their
> meaning.

Sentenzia here means the principle of narrative coherence that orders the temporal mass of the past and places its events on a linear and teleological trajectory.[5] But where does meaning in this sense come from? What is it that gives the author access to the *sentenzia* of those events he finds in his memory? Only now are we in a position to see what is at stake in the proem. A past event receives its meaning from the outcome it contributes to bring about.[6] What confers such meaning is the end that contains the totality of these events in its terminal configuration. Events within a narrative configuration become dense with significance by virtue of this terminal containment. Or, reversing the terms, one could say that only because narrative implies an end does it represent the stronghold of "meaning" in the most basic sense.[7]

In light of the temporal integration projected by the last chapter, it becomes clear that the prose dimension of the *Vita Nuova* already embodies the new manner of representation envisioned by the author. This prose dimension, with its projective, narrative character, signals the beginning of the new project. Its hypothetical character, in the deep sense, embodies a vision of time as a continuity projected unto an outstanding, ultimate outcome. In this sense the prose already belongs to that posthumous language—posthumous to the lyric—envisioned by Dante in the last chapter.[8] We must read the narrative of the *Vita Nuova*, therefore, not just as a veil for Dante's "essayistic statement of poetics," nor merely as a running commentary on the poems, but as an embodiment of the new narrative poetics that somehow announces and ushers in his literary future. That future has already happened. The *libello* comes to us from out of it, in the narrative's forward recollection of the past.

One of the distinctive features of the prose is its moments of silence; these are not moments of reticence, with the author holding back his speech, but of silence in the sense of the still-undisclosed dimensions of the story. The futurity that claims the work as a whole pervades these moments of silence. The last chapter in itself represents a vow of silence on Dante's part, and the fact that he does not describe the content of the miraculous vision underscores his ultimate commitment to silence. Likewise the death of Beatrice, as we have seen, marks a conspicuous moment of authorial silence, indicating once again that the *sentenzia* of that event has yet to be revealed or fulfilled. But do we not return, through the relay of these silences—the death of Beatrice, the last vision—to what I earlier called the genetic secret of the *Vita Nuova*, namely, the marvelous vision of chapter III? "Lo verace giudicio del detto sogno non fue veduto allora d'alcuno, ma ora è manifestissimo a li più semplici." What does Dante mean by this declaration and why does he remain silent about the meaning of the dream? The statement insists on what has become clear to us only now, namely, that time is disclosive of meaning. Visions, as Singleton reminds us, are forward-looking; their meaning attends upon the disclosures of time. The veil that prohibits a view of the dream's meaning—and of the body of Beatrice—is first and foremost the veil of time concealing the future from view. We have spoken about veils in many ways—as Beatrice's phenomenality, as figures and tropes, as the fabric of representation, as the language of allegory, as authentic image—but we are now in a position to understand the degree to which the veil figures as the fabric of temporality itself. The future withheld behind the veil comes to meet us from the veil's recess. This is the same future out of which the book of memory is written.

The association that links time with the veil is by no means foreign to Dante. It has been shown with rare lucidity how the veil of allegory—the "velame de li versi strani"—is unavoidably

linked to the rhetoric of temporality in Dante's *Commedia*.[9] But
the association is perhaps most powerful and explicit in canto
XXXIII of the *Inferno*, where Ugolino recounts the dream that
disclosed the dreadful future to him:

> Breve pertugio dentro da la Muda
> la qual per me ha 'l titol de la fame,
> e'n che conviene ancor ch'altrui si chiuda,
>   m'avea mostrato per lo suo forame
> più lune già, quand' io feci 'l mal sonno
> *che del futuro mi squarciò 'l velame.*
>
> (LL. 22–27)

> A narrow window in the Eagles' Tower,
> which now, through me, is called Hunger Tower,
> a cage in which still others will be locked,
>   had, through its opening, already showed me
> several moons, when I dreamed that bad dream
> *which rent the veil of the future for me.*

Taken as a figure for the veil of time, the *drappo sanguigno*
that covers the body of Beatrice in Dante's "marvelous vision"
accounts for the vision's resistance to explanation at the time of
its occurrence. Its meaning vanishes forward, extends into the
future, opening up a visionary space of presence where presence
points beyond itself toward the terminal ends of the protagonist's destiny.

What, then, has become of the body of Beatrice by the end
of the *libello*? By virtue of its disappearance, it has become an
index of the transcendence of presence—the transcendence by
virtue of which Dante's own futurity inhabits the heart of presence. From the moment Beatrice consumes the flaming heart,
presence passes over into futurity and futurity into presence.
Whereas in the "marvelous vision" a noumenal vision of Beatrice was denied, the last chapter of the *libello* alludes to a truly
noumenal vision of Beatrice in her glory. Where Beatrice resides, and where Dante hopes to arrive once he says of her what

has never been said of any woman, is the noumenal sphere of God's eternal and totalized view of all things in their ontological truth.[10]

And what has become of the crimson veil? We have seen that this is no ordinary veil that merely conceals or covers up; one does not see through it because it is rent the way Ugolino sees through the rent veil of his future. The crimson veil reveals an image of that which it veils, like the Veronica that receives an imprint from the face it has touched. What, then, has become of this veil? It has become the fabric of the *Vita Nuova* which, in its narrative projection unto a terminal end, receives and reveals an imprint of the author's temporal destiny.

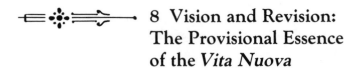 8 Vision and Revision:
The Provisional Essence
of the *Vita Nuova*

To this day the philological controversy over the ending of the *Vita Nuova* remains unresolved. Ever since Luigi Pietrobono, early in the century, proposed his theory of the *rifacimento*—the theory that Dante revised or altered the ending of the *libello* late in his life—scholars have kept the debate alive with periodic attempts to confirm, reject, or modify the thesis.[1] But for every new perspective or piece of evidence that promises a breakthrough, counter-arguments are proposed which keep the question in suspension. "Quel rompicapo della fine della *Vita Nuova*," Maria Corti calls it,[2] for it is the *ending* of the work which gives rise to the problems (how could it be otherwise?). What is the controversy about, and how does it introduce a new dimension to the speculations of the previous chapter?

The problems revolve around the figure of the *donna gentile*. Dante, we recall, encounters her in chapter xxxv, shortly after the first anniversary of Beatrice's death (Beatrice died in June 1290, and Dante's text is traditionally dated around the years 1292–93). The *Vita Nuova* recounts how Dante began to fall in love with this woman but then, after reaffirming his allegiance to the memory of Beatrice, repudiated her. Years later, however, this woman reappears in the *Convivio* as an allegory for Lady Philosophy and as the heroine of Dante's new love of knowledge. There is no doubt about the intertextual identity of the woman:

> I say that the planet of Venus had twice revolved in
> that orbit which makes it appear both in the evening
> and the morning, after the passing of the blessed

Beatrice who lives in heaven with the angels and on earth in my soul, when that gentle lady, whom I speak about at the end of the *Vita nuova*, first appeared to my eyes, accompanied by Love, and occupied a place in my mind. (*Convivio*, II. 2. 1).

The first big problem created by this intertextual identity is that the *donna gentile* appears here in the role of heroine with no explanation of, or reference to, the fact that the author had previously overcome the "malicious desire and vain temptation" of this new love. Furthermore, if we chart the temporal coordinates offered by Dante in this passage (he uses a system of astronomical calculation derived from Alfraganus), the date he proposes for his first encounter with the lady is 1293. This means that a period of more than two years had elapsed between the first anniversary of Beatrice's death and the encounter, which means, in turn, that a temporal gap of more than two years obtains between chapters xxxiv and xxxv of the *Vita Nuova*. Is this possible? In the latter chapter, Dante uses the phrase "alquanto tempo" to describe the lapse of time in question—a phrase used often in the work to refer to minutes and hours, and sometimes to days, but never to a substantial length of time like months or years.[3]

The most intriguing aspect of the *Convivio* passage, however, is Dante's comment about the woman "whom I speak about at the end of the *Vita nuova*" [*quella gentile donna, cui feci menzione a la fine della Vita nuova*]. Lexical surveys of the word *fine* in Dante's corpus have shown that Dante never employs the word loosely but only in reference to the termination of something. But in the version of the *Vita Nuova* that we possess (which, by the way, is the same version Boccaccio knew), there are four full chapters and three sonnets that follow the episode of the *donna gentile* before the work comes to an end. Could Dante have had this ending in mind when he wrote the *Convivio*? Unless this is Dante's one and only aberrant use of the word *fine*, it seems highly unlikely.[4]

Finally, in the *Vita Nuova* Dante tells us that his flirtation with the woman lasted "alquanto die"—a few days—but according to the *Convivio*, this new love had a duration of some years (the famous period of the "trenta mesi," II. 12. 1–9).

Discrepancies of this sort are what gave rise to theories of a later revision of the *libello*'s ending. The theories are diverse and at times as nebulous as Dante's own autobiographical remarks, but in order to give them weight let me simply propose what I take to be a highly plausible scenario. Let us imagine a prior version of the *Vita Nuova* which ended with the author's new love for philosophy in the allegorical figure of the *donna gentile*. This is far from inconceivable. We know that Dante was still mourning Beatrice at the time and that he had begun to read Boethius's *Consolation of Philosophy* shortly after her death. We also know that in the early work the *donna gentile* appears unequivocally as a figure of consolation, whether or not she was intended allegorically.[5] But let us entertain Dante's remarks in the *Convivio* that the *donna gentile* is and always was an allegory for Lady Philosophy. In that case the *Vita Nuova* would originally have ended with Dante's *consolation for the death of Beatrice in his immersion in philosophy*. This would be consistent with the biography, and it would certainly have allowed Dante to maintain a narrative intrigue in his *libello*, an intrigue created by a transfer of affections away from Beatrice which gets resolved by an unexpected revelation: that the new love is not a woman at all, but rather philosophy. This new love could then be reconciled with the memory of Beatrice (after all, the *libello* insists from the beginning on the role played by the "consiglio de la ragione" in the poet's love for Beatrice), and the story would terminate in a grand fashion with the author once again in his study, but this time holding hands with Lady Philosophy. An original version of the *Vita Nuova* along these lines is not only conceivable but ultimately highly plausible.

Let us go on to imagine another highly plausible scenario, namely, that once Dante gave up the *Convivio*, abandoning both the project and his love affair with philosophy, he returned to the earlier work and changed its ending to render it consistent with his vision of a wholly new project, for example, the *Commedia*. Thus, instead of the consoling triumph of the *donna gentile* and her allegorical reconciliation with the memory of Beatrice, Dante introduces into the narrative a repudiation of the new love and a renewed allegiance to Beatrice herself, with a promise to write of her more worthily (an implicit and subtle act of contrition for having looked to philosophy for consolation). In other words, the same reconsiderations that would have induced Dante to revise the early work after the *Convivio* would also have caused him to view it as an inadequate treatment of Beatrice. This too would be consistent with what we know about Dante's reasons for abandoning the *Convivio* (and the consolation of philosophy) and embarking upon the *Commedia*.

I have described my own reconstruction of what I take to be the most credible working hypothesis in this "giallo," or mystery story, as Corti calls it. But the fact that I personally suspect Dante returned to the *Vita Nuova* later in life and revised it along these lines does not help in the philological search for evidence. To be sure, the protagonists of the controversy have generously indulged in hypothetical speculation themselves, but the issue must be decided ultimately on the basis of evidence, which means, in effect, that it will most likely never be decided. The burden of proof naturally falls on those who uphold the *rifacimento* theory. When Pietrobono first proposed the theory, Michele Barbi reacted with a hard-nosed challenge based on the fact that the oldest manuscripts of the *Vita Nuova* show no trace of any such *rifacimento*.[6] But Barbi was unruffled by the fact that our oldest manuscripts date back only to the fourteenth century, and he had the confidence or complacency to declare, "To me it seems a lack of critical sagacity to rely on the affirmations of the *Convivio*, whether chronological or other, to illuminate the episode of the 'donna pietosa' of the *Vita nuova*. Just as the affirmations of the philosophical work are not enough to make me believe that that episode is allegorical, so the chronological indications of the two orbits of Venus and the thirty months (*Conv.*, II. 2. 1 and XII. 1–9) do not persuade me that [the affair] lasted that long."[7] It was Olympian attitudes of this sort toward the discrepancies in Dante's texts which inspired Bruno Nardi to ask, in the title of an essay that marked his entrance into the controversy on the side of the *rifacimento* theory, "S'ha da credere a Dante o ai suoi critici?" ["Are we to believe Dante or his critics?"].[8] In any case, the controversies of Pietrobono/Barbi and Barbi/Nardi are some of the more amusing episodes in recent Dante scholarship for their almost parodic parade of an Italian academic style, a style that would seem to be vanishing among present-day Italian *dantisti*, who can now look back on those episodes with a degree of cynicism.[9]

In 1965 Mario Marti tried to settle the *rifacimento* matter once and for all with a new piece of philological evidence. He proved that "Oltre la spera," the last sonnet of the *Vita Nuova*, was composed *before* the years 1303–4. His evidence came from two sonnets addressed to Dante by the poet Cecco Angiolieri. The first of these was composed before the two poets broke off their friendship, and in it Cecco asks Dante to elucidate "Oltre la spera," which Cecco had found obscure. While this first sonnet ("Alighier, Cecco il tu' servo e amico") cannot be dated with precision, the second poem addressed to Dante ("Dante Alighier, s'i' son ben begolardo"), which Cecco composed after the rupture, can be assigned a relatively precise date, for it makes reference to Dante having become a "Lombardo." Dante first traveled to Lombardy in 1303–4, where he enjoyed the hospitality of Bartolomeo della Scala. Marti argued that since Cecco's second sonnet could not have been composed later than 1304, Dante's "Oltre la spera" was certainly composed before that date.[10]

For Marti this meant the conclusive "death" of the *rifacimento* theory, but Maria Corti has reopened the debate once again:

Apart from the excessive chronological rigor of Marti
(the second sonnet could date from 1304 and the first
slightly earlier), and apart from the possibility of
Dante's insertion of a poem composed earlier into the
Vita Nuova (had he not done so with the poems of the
Vita Nuova and the allegorical *canzoni* of the Con-
vivio?), there are also certain linguistic clues, certain
lexical and stylistic features, that is to say textual
and therefore unequivocal features, that I would like
to present, since they seem to complicate the provocative mystery story [*giallo*] of the end of the *Vita
Nuova*.[11]

Corti goes on to disclose Dante's unequivocal use of the word
fine, his invocation of a specific text of Aristotle's toward the
end of the Vita Nuova (there is no indication earlier in the work
that he had read Aristotle), and his plea to God in the last
chapter that his life may last a few more years ("che la mia vita
duri alquanti anni"), a plea that seems unusual, to say the least,
for a twenty-eight-year-old man, though not so unusual if
Dante composed this chapter some fifteen or sixteen years later.
But despite her sympathies for the *rifacimento* theory (Nardi was
after all her *maestro*), Corti stresses that problems persist on either side of the issue, leaving us with what amounts to an insoluble enigma: "What is certain," she declares, "is that we do not
escape from the conditional mood" (p. 155).

What is at stake in the controversy apart from our historical curiosity about the facts? At this point perhaps the failures
of philology to account for the facts once and for all must become a matter for hermeneusis. Perhaps something about the
Vita Nuova conspires with the empirical uncertitudes to frustrate attempts to bring the work to chronological closure. It is
not by chance that the problems revolve around the ending(s)
of the narrative. In a work that is projective in character—
whose end announces a beginning and whose "memory" is in
every sense futural—in a work that makes vision an essential

mode of temporal anticipation, perhaps revision is more than a matter of dates or facts, and becomes instead a constitutive narrative as well as an existential category. We do not have to decide the issue of *rifacimento*, we have only to concede its possibility in order to see that revision remains a fundamental and always already operative principle of the *libello*. The possibility of a later revision, in other words, remains plausible because of the revisionary agenda that sustains the work. The structural adjacency of poems and prose—the schizoid *prosimetrum* genre—in itself signals this revisionary agenda. And what does the "story" dramatize if not a series of corrections and revisions in the poet's search for an adequate idiom? In how many cases does the protagonist revise his behavior in the story? The case of the screen ladies; the change of strategy after Beatrice denies her greetings; the peripeteia of the *donna gentile*; the encounter with the pilgrims; the great revision, finally, of the miraculous vision. The fact that the work as we know it ends with a totalized revision of the literary project as Dante had conceived it up until that point only crystallizes the logic of transcendence that has sustained the narrative all along.

What seems necessary, therefore, is a reinscription of the philological debate within this greater horizon of transcendence which claims the narrative from the very beginning. Ideally the ending of such a work should be infinitely revisable from the perspective of the future into which it extends prophetically, as it were, in the mode of vision. What is clear is that Dante's career is characterized by a pattern of revisionary transcendence, of self-correction and self-revisitation as a way of moving forward. With every palinode, with every progressive step of self-transcendence from the perspective of which the past is subjected to an immanent critique, with every *turn away* that also involves a *turn toward*, we witness in Dante's subsequent career the extent to which the idea of a *vita nuova* functions as a regulative idea. In this sense *vita nuova* means open to revision.

If the visionary futurity of the *Vita Nuova* implies its "retroactive realignment of the past," then these two dimensions together—the visionary and the revisionary, the projective and the recollective, the attentive and the retentive—have their grounding in the *pro-visionary* essence of the artifact. There is a difference, however, between the work's provisionary essence and its provisional character. Its provisional character derives from the author's avowed goal to write a more valid book sometime in the future. Its provisionary essence, on the other hand, derives from the particular configuration of human temporality which underlies its visions and revisions and informs its narrative logic.

To an overwhelming extent, scholars have been preoccupied with the provisional character of the work. Its open-endedness has led to an almost irresistible compulsion to read it against the background of Dante's later works, above all the *Commedia*.[12] This is of course only natural in the case of an author who not only gave a wholly proleptic aspect to his first work but went on to write a momentous masterpiece. But what would happen if we put brackets around the author's subsequent career, indeed, around the author himself, and looked at the *Vita Nuova* as a work without sequence? How then would things stand with the *libello*? They would stand in the suspense of the last chapter: a critical "meantime" between past and future. And what if we asked about the essence of that meantime which turns the last chapter into a critical mass, a dense configuration of grammatical tenses and moods, a strange silence pregnant with future speech? Is this a meantime on a chronological trajectory—the year 1292, ten years before the *Commedia*—or is the threshold at which the protagonist arrives here one at which human temporality always already finds itself at any moment in time? What if the *Vita Nuova*, at its deepest level, ends not on a chronological trajectory at all but in the midst of human finitude, at a temporal edge beyond which the rest is hypothetical? It seems indispensable in concluding this investigation to come to terms with the provisionary essence of the *libello*. This, in turn, means emancipating it from the name of its author.

In what follows I do not presume to expound what the author had or thought he had or intended for us to have in mind when he composed the *libello*. I am interested rather in the untold story: a story that tells the story of stories and that to some extent escapes authorial intentions.

The Existential Subjunctive

It is essential to narratives that they attain closure in an end, for they are determined from the start by the logic of such closure. The *Vita Nuova* is an unusual text in this regard, for it at once confirms and defies the logic of narrative closure. It confirms that logic to the extent that, through the miraculous vision, Dante envisions a linear existential trajectory that ends in conjunction with the beatific order to which Beatrice belongs and in which she waits for him to speak of her adequately. By ending with a vision of a totalized end from the perspective of which existential time assumes a narrative order, the *Vita Nuova* tells the story of Dante's *discovery* of narrative time, over against lyric time, for instance. Thus, the teleological projections that articulate the last chapter confirm the logic of narrative closure. At the same time, we cannot ignore the fact that, as a story about the poet's experimentations, ventures, and quests, the *Vita Nuova* simply fails to come to an end. It remains profoundly "unfinished," and yet this unfinishedness gives coherence to the work as a whole. How can this be? How can the last chapter represent both a hyper-end and a pseudo-end? How does it manage to subvert narrative logic at the very moment it discovers it?

There is no great mystery here. The projection of a hypothetical end, not yet realized or attained in narrative time, allows the *libello* to remain unfinished and yet contained within the parameters of narrative closure that it envisions for itself. Hypothetical projection is the enabling element of the last chapter. It is by virtue of, and it is *in*, such projection that the work comes to an end. But what does this mean? We have already seen that the *libello*'s projective drive is itself grounded in the revelations of the miraculous vision, and that projection therefore is *not* the primordial element. Likewise we have seen that through the agency of the vision existential time receives its measure from the eternal order. There is strong evidence, in any case, that something of this sort takes place in the last chapter, and to expound the logic of conjunction whereby existential time derives its measure from the eternal contributes a significant insight into the essence of the *libello*. However, the last chapter also tells another story, for it conceals a tension beween the paradigm articulated so far and what I have called the provisionary essence of the work.

Throughout this study I have emphasized the phenomenality of Beatrice: the veils that adorn her, conceal her, and yet render her accessible to both perception and poetic praise. I have tried to show that in Dante's conversion to Beatrice there exists a tension toward a withdrawing body, a noumenal entity that, as it withdraws, offers its presence to Dante in phenomenal, figurative, "poetic" guises. I have also been at pains to correlate the phenomenality of Beatrice with temporality. Beatrice's phenomenality is the mark of her transience. As we saw in the case of "Tanto gentile," she passes by. In another case, that of the marvelous vision, she withdraws behind her crimson veil toward the sky, just as the dream's *verace giudicio* recedes into the future, inscrutable to those who attempted to explain it at the time. Her death is merely the consummation of her phenomenality, and hence her temporality. The noumenal dimension of Beatrice—her body in Dante's dream, her glory in heaven's realm, her ontological truth in God's all-seeing eye—this noumenal dimension of Beatrice is correlated to God's eternal order. Or at least it would seem that way. The last chapter of the *Vita Nuova* actually alludes to a noumenal vision of Beatrice. It brings the narrative to an abrupt end by vouching for the primacy of the noumenal over the phenomenal, of the eternal over the temporal, of the configurational over the episodic, and we are left with the author's declaration that his resources are still unequal to the revelations of the miraculous vision. And yet this voucher remains suspect. The *Vita Nuova* cannot honor it. In spite of the authorial intentions to affirm the contrary, Dante's *libello* in fact reveals that the eternal has its source in human temporality, and not the other way around. How so?

Let us look again at how the miraculous vision inaugurates and yet cuts short the story. The narrative description of its occurrence seems ordinary enough: "Appresso questo sonnetto apparve a me una mirabile visione" ["After this sonnet there appeared to me a miraculous vision"]. The vision takes its place within the chronological, episodic sequence of "this happened, then that happened, and then that happened," which is to say the narrative sequence. It interrupts this sequence, to be sure, but we have seen that it also allows the author, for the first time, to envision a narrative configuration in the otherwise indifferent chronology of sequence. However, what Dante emphasizes most about the vision is its direct, unmediated effect on his own secular activity: ". . . una mirabile visione ne la quale io vidi cose *che mi fecero* proporre di non dire più di questa benedetta fino a quando non potessi più degnamente trattare di lei." The author's literary project takes over the meaning of the vision at the very moment that he attains access to meaning (the *sentenzia* of the new life). This incorporation on the existential level gives the vision a wholly lateral extension. The vision *is*, in a sense, a vision of the enterprise that lies ahead of the author, in his secular future.

Now the several ambiguities and paradoxes of the last chapter derive ultimately from the fact that the miraculous vision has happened and has not yet happened. It has happened insofar as a projection of goals takes place in the last chapter; it has not happened insofar as a *second* vision at the end of the existential trajectory must eventually fulfill its meaning. This supplementary role of the postponed second vision points to the true hypothetical nature of the first. The miraculous vision becomes a prodigious hypothesis of a hyperbole, namely, Dante's ultimate noumenal vision of Beatrice at the end of his new life: "che la mia anima possa gire a vedere la gloria della sua donna." What sort of hypothetical projection is this? Where does it receive its stimulus? Does it come from the miraculous vision itself or from the author's hope, which stretches him forward in the mode of desire? Where, in other words, does the *Vita Nuova* end?

What gives the work a meaningful "end," in the narrative sense, is not so much the provisional conclusion of the story but the *existential subjunctive* of the last chapter. The term refers to a particular temporal phenomenon. The *libello* ends in the subjunctive mood. I do not mean this only in the grammatical sense, though we have seen how many of the verbs in the last chapter are indeed in the subjunctive mood, but more in the sense of the author's self-extention into the future in the mode of desire, hope, or expectation. The existential subjunctive is expressed in the reference of the *that*: I wish *that*, I hope *that*. The *that* opens up a specific temporal horizon. In this respect the two main verbs in the present indicative—"io spero" and "io studio"—are wholly subjunctive in character. "Io spero" relates the author to his future in the mode of desire; likewise, "io studio" invokes the future as something one awaits with eagerness. Etymologically, "to study" means nothing less than "to desire, to be eager for." Hence the present tense of narrative time—which, as we have seen, articulates the narrative configuration—is actually a subjunctive veil through which the future shows its hypothetical face.

To resolve upon a goal in hope and eagerness and to refer the past forward toward that goal amount to the existential subjunction, or joining together (*sub-iungere*), of past and present with the future, the future from which time as a whole receives its openness as well as its possibility for closure. By virtue of the existential subjunctive, the future reveals itself as something that has already happened and yet not happened, that is to say as something that is somehow already operative in the various thresholds of the past which brought the protagonist to the threshold of the narrative present. Eternity is but a provisionary expectation, a subjunctive hypothesis, in the space opened up by the immanent finitude of time. The provisionary essence of the *Vita Nuova* lies in the revelation that existential time takes its measure *not* from the eternal but rather from its own inner transcendence as a being unto the future. This inner transcendence, which brings the future back into past and present time, keeps human time under the governance of finitude and yet beyond the law of mere chronological time. It is the enabling condition for a narrative configuration of time, and as Dante discovers the logic of narrative in the *Vita Nuova*, so too he points to the finite transcendence of a merely human temporality.

In his last chapter Dante declares that he hopes his life will last a few more years (a temporal expectation), in which case he hopes to say of Beatrice what has never been said of any woman (a temporal expectation), and that he hopes, finally, that his soul may see her in her glory (a temporal expectation of the ultimate transcendence of time). If a noumenal vision is its ultimate and postponed possibility, we must call the *Vita Nuova* provisionary in essence, for it looks forward not only to an ultimate vision but also to a hypothetical end that *it engenders* from out of its own existential dynamism. Pro-vision thus becomes primordial. It comes first. It remains prior to vision, and not the other way around. In this sense the entire visionary mode of the *Vita Nuova*, in which the protagonist's phenomenal perceptions tend toward the withdrawing noumenal mysteries of Beatrice, remains provisionary. But we may now say that neither is pro-vision merely a preview of vision, nor phenomenal perception merely an incomplete, deprived version of noumenal perception. On the contrary, the dream of the noumenal arises from the finite epiphanies of Beatrice's phenomenality, just as the dream of some hyperbolic and ultimate vision of her in her glory arises from the inner, open-ended transcendence of human temporality.

"Quel rompicapo della fine della *Vita Nuova*." I have tried to show here that there are transphilological reasons why the ending of the *Vita Nuova* remains an insoluble chronological enigma for philology: it is an ending that grounds chronological time in the deeper structures of hypothetical time, out of which narrative time assumes its particular configuration. And if Maria Corti is right to say that "we do not escape from the conditional mood" when we talk about the end of the *Vita Nuova*, is this not also and above all because the work ends not so much on a chronological trajectory but in the finitude of provisionary time, which keeps the dream of closure open?

 **Epilogue**

Francesca

You came in out of the night
And there were flowers in your hands,
Now you will come out of a confusion of people,
Out of a turmoil of speech about you.

I who have seen you amid the primal things
Was angry when they spoke your name
In ordinary places.
I would that the cool waves might flow over my mind,
And that the world should dry as a dead leaf,
Or as a dandelion seedpod and be swept away,
So that I might find you again,
Alone.

Ezra Pound, Personae, 1908–10

And then went down to the ship,
Set keel to breakers, forth on the godly sea, and
We set up mast and sail on that swart ship,
Bore sheep aboard her, and our bodies also
Heavy with weeping, and winds from sternward
Bore us out onward with bellying canvas,
Circe's this craft, the trim-coifed goddess.

Ezra Pound, Cantos, I, 1–7 (1930)

What does it mean when a lyric poet decides to assume an
epic voice? In some cases it means that the poet is intent on
becoming a point of conjunction in tradition, a savior of the

"and" that assures transcendent continuities between historical epochs. The conspicuous grammatical conjunctions in the opening verses of Ezra Pound's first Canto very nearly sum up the story of this kind of epic ambition. For Pound the turn toward the epic enterprise meant an attempt to go beyond a merely "personal" voice in order to embark, in the plural, upon a wider horizon of literary and ideological relevance. His efforts led to a veritable misadventure, but the ultimate shipwreck of the *Cantos* nevertheless reveals the degree to which the epoch found its reflection no longer in epic totalities but rather in the fragmentation or liquidation of the epic project as such.

What was Pound's renunciation of the lyric all about? Why did he turn against Francesca, so to speak, or in any case give up the hope of finding her again, alone? To find Francesca again, alone, is the intimate and nuclear dream of the personal lyric. The prospect of such a recovery lures the lyric subject with the promise of overcoming, at long last, the common and communal world where names are spoken in a great Babelonian confusion of people and fallen speech. Francesca's proper name cannot, or should not, be spoken in "ordinary places," for it belongs not to the world but to the edenic and private property of lyric experience. Its inscription in the title of Pound's poem refers to the memory of primal things, before Francesca's name fell from the plenitude of private vision into the turmoil of a public world.

Some experience, some vision, some epiphany of presence has already happened—Francesca has already come in out of the night, Beatrice has already greeted her lover, God has already become man—some event has already taken place, and the labor thereafter is to recover the extraordinary fact of its occurrence. Ultimately the ordinary figures simply as a lack of poetic vision. Those who speak Francesca's name in ordinary places do not or cannot see her amid the primal things. Speech in this sense is intimately linked to vision. But after that first unlikely occurrence, the poet too loses the epiphany of poetic vision. The public world exists to trouble it. A cool wave does not wash over the lyric mind or consign to oblivion the community of the ordinary, nor does the world dry up like a dead leaf and leave the poet face to face with Francesca again. The commotions and disarrays of history keep lyric experience on this side of a purged privacy. In Pound's case the Great War offered an abundant spectacle of the world's communal and infernal passions:

> There died a myriad,
> And of the best, among them,
> For an old bitch gone in the teeth,
> For a botched civilization,
>
> Charm, smiling at the good mouth,
> Quick eyes gone under earth's lid,
>
> For two gross of broken statues,
> For a few thousand battered books.
>   "Hugh Selwyn Mauberley," pt. 5 [1920]

Among the myriad, "of the best," there died several of Pound's generation: poets and artists, men his own age or younger, in any case young men losing their voices in the infernal trenches "for a few thousand battered books." How, then, does the survivor of a generation of lost voices speak? What vision will now generate speech? Can the poet any longer presume to speak Francesca's name again, alone? What can the obsession with personal salvation mean when history has undone so many? Musn't the botched civilization, the few thousand books, be redeemed for the very sake of the unredeemed "under earth's lid"? And doesn't the work of redemption begin by saving the "and" that keeps the story going? At a certain point it may dawn on a poet that salvation is no longer a personal affair but a historical narrative in crisis, a narrative of the confusions of people and turmoils of speech. The poet—Ezra Pound in this case—does not give up his personal love but globalizes it. The project of a lyric recovery gives way to that of a universal reappropriation of the public domain. The epic alternative. When a lyric poet suspects that Francesca can no longer be found again alone, but must be found again communally, a search for the epic voice seems a likely alternative.

What does this mean? In the first place it means that the poet embarks, in one form or another, on a voyage to the underworld—the place of the myriad—where he undertakes to give voice to the dead. To save the dead from speechlessness becomes the first step in the epic enterprise of redemption. Thus, a collective generation is made to speak again in and through the poet's monumental labor of prosopopoeia, which is no longer the prosopopoeia of a lyric voice but rather the prosopopoeia of a voice of "tradition" which gives speech to the collective dead. Every such epic journey involves a descent into the underworld and a transfer of the living voice to the dead. The dead now register their grievances in a warning to the world to reform its wayward course and to restore history to its sanity. Thus they dispose of the poet's verbal vitality in order to reverse the terms of their damnation.

One could say, then, that in the final analysis the only essential change when a lyric poet chooses the epic alternative is the magnitude of the voice's resonance. For Pound the turn to the *Cantos* meant a turn to a more exalted order of lyricism, an even more personal ritual of confession. The voyage from private nostalgia to epic globality does not entail a greater reconciliation on the poet's part to the world's public history; on the contrary, it entails a denunciation of public history in the name of some extraordinary ideal order of meaning that history should follow. In Pound's case the lyric desire to hold the world at bay merely gives way to an aggressive confrontation with the world's turmoil in the hope of bringing about a revaluation of values, so to speak. The new epic voice now presumes to speak as the guardian of the founding values of the tribe and to redefine them over against the worldly fallenness of history.[1]

How do such epic confrontations end? Every epoch contains its own possibilities for ends and endings. The fragments that announce the end of Pound's *Cantos* offer an unsettling

ceremony of confession on the part of a poet who failed to recover the higher lyricism of Francesca for the communal world
at large. They are fragments that reveal the possibilities and im-
possibilities inherent in an epoch that broods over ends and
endings but that itself does not know how to come to an end:

> M'amour, m'amour
>> what do I love and
>>> where are you?
> That I lost my center
>> fighting the world.
> The dreams clash
>> and are shattered—
> and that I tried to make a paradiso
>> terrestre.

* * * * *

> I have tried to write Paradise
> Do not move
>> Let the wind speak
>>> that is paradise.
> Let the Gods forgive what I
>> have made
> Let those I love try to forgive
>> what I have made.

When Dante enters into the earthly paradise in *Purgatorio*
xxvIII, he finds himself alone with his Francesca. Her name is
Matelda. She too bears flowers in her hands as she stands on
the bank of the river Lethe—the "cool wave" of Pound's poem
that would flow over the lyric mind and bring forgetfulness of
the fallen world. Dante sees her amid the primal things: birds,
flowers, the noon sun, the spring season. She represents a supreme lyric fantasy.[2] Perhaps for that reason the private encounter with Matelda cannot last but must give way to the ceremonious, allegorical, and epic advent of Beatrice on the

opposite bank of the river. The pastoral moment gives way to the boisterous procession of the chariot and griffin, the seven candlesticks, the twenty-four old men, the four animals, and so on, and the poet who for a moment found Matelda now loses her again as Beatrice moralizes and institutionalizes his entrance into the *paradiso terrestre*. The conspicuous delyricization of Beatrice here is both unsettling and thought-provoking. One is tempted to believe that she actually remains veiled in the figure of Matelda, and that the triumphant soul who appears at the head of the allegorical pageantry is merely a necessary fiction of the *Divine Comedy*.

From the perspective of this study, the appearance of Beatrice in the earthly paradise is painfully ironic, for at the very moment that he has her pronounce his name and publicly accuse him of having betrayed her memory, Dante betrays the Beatrice who greeted him one day on the streets of Florence. Whereas in the *Vita Nuova* the poet never presumed to lend voice to Beatrice but insisted that his own speech remained beholden to her vital inspirations, in *Purgatorio* xxx it is the poet who, in a singular act of self-confidence, lends speech to Beatrice through ventriloquistic powers of prosopopoeia. The redemption of her memory in the epic enterprise turns out, from another perspective, to be the ultimate demise of that memory.

But at the same time we are forced to ask whether the contiguity of Beatrice and Matelda in the earthly paradise does not point to a deeper coincidence or intersection between the lyric and the epic impulse in Dante's career. While it certainly dramatizes a difference between the nostalgias of lyricism and the inexorable processions of epic, it also reveals the underlying complicity that links them to one another, for this transfigured Beatrice who comes to bring an end to the idyllic moment of lyric indulgence has merely become the agent of a higher lyricism, an epic lyricism, if one may call it that. Her purpose is to lead Dante to a vision of the celestial rose and, ultimately, to a beatific vision of the Christian God. In one form or another the epic vision that brings closure to Dante's journey has its distant origin in the provisionary impulse of his early lyric experience. It is not by chance that a distinct lyric mode takes over Dante's poem when he approaches the upper reaches of his *Paradiso*, as if to suggest that the *Commedia* were nothing less than a sublime consummation of lyric nostalgia.

One could say, then, that the fragmentations and confessions of failure that bring Pound's *Cantos* to an end figure as a negative or aborted version of the beatific vision that gives Dante's epic a comic closure. Contrary to Pound, but in the same vein as Pound, Dante in some way *finds* his center fighting the world, writing his Paradise without appeals for forgiveness. But his successful "completion" of the *Commedia* as opposed to Pound's fragmentations of the *Cantos* remains in the final analysis only an epochal difference. There are other important differences between the failure of one enterprise and the success of the other, to be sure, but these differences remain grounded in a deeper lyric identity.

Seen retrospectively and from the perspective of Dante's future poetics, the *Vita Nuova* ends somewhere in the empty space between the lyric and epic options that circumscribe his career as a whole. Lying just beyond their identities and differences, it confronts us with the enigma of its unresolved quest for a literary alternative. Expressed succinctly and essentially and from my own perspective, the *libello* tells a story not about literary alternatives in themselves—poetry/prose, lyric/narrative—but about what is at stake in literary alternatives. I have tried to show that what is at stake for Dante is a relationship to time and its impossible closure. I have tried in this same vein to show that the *Vita Nuova* offers a rare insight into how both the lyric and narrative impulses aspire, in one form or another, to transcendent temporal closure (narrative in this sense is not equivalent to epic but figures as its necessary precondition). While Beatrice lived, she embodied transcendence in the "miraculous" nature of her person, the epideictic lyric flourishing in the sphere of her presence. With her death and disappearance, the lyric voice falls into crisis, falters, reaches an impasse that leads to a totalized revision of the past. The *Vita Nuova* ends with a critical projection toward some eventual transcendent closure of the new life, but in the "meantime" the narrative of crisis remains suspended in the author's contract with the future. I have tried to suggest that the "meantime temporality" of the work engages the terms of human temporality at its most fundamental level. The *libello*, in other words, shows how this temporality not only underlies but even enables the hypothetical projection unto some terminal end. The prophetic mode that sustains Dante's mature work, as well as the ideologies it endorses, have as their precondition this specific ecstatic temporality, that is to say, a temporality in need of, but ultimately denied, closure. To that extent one could say that the *Vita Nuova* probes the preconditions of both Dante's lyric past and his epic future. The provisional "meantime" to which it belongs makes the work an implicit and perhaps even inadvertent demystification of the impulse that sustains both the lyric and epic alternatives. In other words, it reveals the nostalgic nature of this impulse as well as the dreams of salvation to which it gives rise.

In an early and little-known piece, Michel Foucault comments on the relation between dreams and the meaning of history in terms that are potentially fruitful here: "Not that dreams are the truth of history, but, causing the eruption of that in existence which is most irreducible to history, they show better than all else the meaning history can assume for a freedom which has not yet attained the moment of its universality in objective expression."[3] A dream or vision that is irreducible to history—Francesca amid the primal things, Beatrice in a crimson cloth—a dream or vision in its very irreducibility to history, enables the poet to reappropriate the meaning of history in the freedom of poetic expression. But this same freedom enables the epic poet to construe the *meaning* of history over against the *truth* of history. The epic enterprise, which engages and, in Dante's and Pound's cases, challenges history, becomes a great dream of the meaning of history: a dream that can never coincide with the truth of history precisely because it is irreducible to history.

But Foucault's remark that dreams are not the truth of history can be reconceived in a shift of terms that would state: "history is not the truth of dreams." This simple reversal would warn us that the meaning of a dream cannot come from an objective confirmation of its visionary foreboding. "The true meaning of this dream was not seen by anyone at the time, but now it is manifest to even the most simple-minded." In an earlier discussion we remarked that "meaning" in this case is a narrative category that makes meaning beholden to futurity. The "true meaning" of this dream, to use Dante's paradoxical phrase, is that the future claims Beatrice as its own and that Dante's finitude finds in her fugitive motion a figure for itself. Whether or not Beatrice dies and "confirms" the forebodings of Dante's marvelous vision is finally irrelevant. Whether or not the "Veltro" comes one day and redeems the prophecy of *Inferno* I is equally irrelevant. Whether or not Dante actually writes of Beatrice what has never been written of any woman is also irrelevant to the promise that ends the *Vita Nuova*. What is not irrelevant is the fact that "meaning"—whether of a vision, the new life, or history as a whole—involves a narrative projection that begins in the eruption of dreams and whose end is given only prophetically. This, then, would be the "meaning" of the *Vita Nuova*.

Dante could not forgive Guido Cavalcanti his disdainful skepticism about the epic attempt to construe universal meaning in the freedom of poetic expression. With his acute analytic phantasmology of the self, Guido understood too much about the impossibility of a synthetic representation of the Real; too much about the seductive edifications of figurative language; too much about the intransitive nature of poetic vision. His psycho-poetry turns the figure back upon itself until it decomposes its own chimeric constitution and reveals its ontological emptiness. Where Dante, in faith and hope, risks the hyperbole and posits the figure in acts of projection, Guido entraps the resources of poetry in the movement of introjection. His refusal of narrativity and his retreat into the private phantasmagoria of psycho-lyricism harbor a denial of the referential possibilities of representation. What can it mean, finally, that Dante dedicated the *Vita Nuova* to this friend?

Guido suffered his whole life from a wound the nature of which remains inscrutable. Dante for some reason could not forgive him that wound, most likely because he believed in a remedy that Guido refused to take seriously. " 'Se per questo cieco / carcere vai per altezza d'ingegno, / mio figlio ov' è? e perché non è teco?' " [" 'If it is your high intellect / that lets you journey here, through this blind prison, / where is my son? Why is he not with you?' "] This is what Guido's father wants to know from Dante in *Inferno* x, in the realm of the heretics. Dante points to his guide and suggests by way of an answer that perhaps Guido's disdain for Virgil explains why he is not on the journey.[4] Much is at stake in that answer, but for us in this discussion it means that a lyric poet—a poet of the self's liquidation and inherent disgrace—refused the epic alternative that Dante presumed to find through his long study of the Virgilian poem.[5] Virgil, the poet of history, empire, and epic, brought about for Dante a reorientation from the personal to the communal, the existential to the historical, the private to the public, in short, the lyric to the epic, and made possible for the first time the transformation of the single self's *vita nuova* into the *nostra vita* of the *Commedia*'s first verse. Guido would not have followed him in that publicization of the voice, perhaps because he belonged to those whom history had defeated. There is a strong sense in *Inferno* x that Dante too numbers himself among the defeated, but unlike Guido (and like Pound), he seemed to believe that the meaning of history could overcome the truth of history. For Dante, Guido's refusal of the hypothetical meant his acceptance of death as an absolute limit. Thus his ghost is evoked in the graveyard of those "che l'anima col corpo morta fanno" ["who say the soul dies with the body"].

What did Petrarch see in all of this a few decades later? He saw much ado about nothing: the nothing that lurks at the heart of time. He saw that in Dante there was a mad hyperbole at work in the theology of poetry and the poetry of theology which brought forth the *Commedia*, a hyperbole that led to a gothic contamination of style in the artifact. Although Petrarch ransacked Dante's *Rime* as well as the *Commedia* for his own vernacular purposes, the stylistic imperative in his case predominated over every other imperative, precisely because style was one's triumph over the nothing. Thus Petrarch defined a wholly different horizon for the personal lyric. His science of style, so to speak, reflects a new sense of measure, humanistic in nature, which commits his lyric to the secular drama of time. The music of his verse is measured by the ticking of a clock, the steady sequence of days, years, anniversaries, and with him the artifice of poetry wins out over its hyperbolic theology.

On the other hand, a deep lyric sympathy links him to Guido, in whom he saw an aristocratic restraint and refinement that he was bound to admire. He believed no doubt that Guido was right about the uncircumscribable limit of personal death, but he did not share the metaphysical anguish, the Averroistic despair, that make so many of Guido's poems a testimony of subjective surrender. Whereas Guido liquidates the substantiality of the self in his psycho-poetry, Petrarch ritualistically recomposes the artifice of the self from out of nothing in his *Canzoniere*. Aestheticism beomes a lucid, unself-deceived, and willful response to the mockery of mortality. What saved Petrarch from Guido's bleeding wound was above all his vanity, as the elegance of lament redeemed the very condition of lament.

But despite their differences, which go beyond mere temperament and point to epochal transformations, both Cavalcanti and the Petrarch of the *Canzoniere* represent cases of lyric stubbornness that sets them off from Dante. Both refused the narrative logic that was the first step in Dante's venture which would eventually lead him beyond the crystalline sphere to a vision of his God. But Dante stands alone not only in this medieval company, but in the history of literature as a whole. There is a mad epic extravagance in Dante that remains altogether unseemly and unearthly. One does not know how to account for its hyperbole. Perhaps we must believe him finally about Beatrice, the woman of the new life. Clearly the genetic secret of his career lay somewhere beyond himself.

Notes

Introduction: Critical Differences

1. For a summary of the controversy and a discussion of its wider implications, see chapter 8.

2. Charles S. Singleton, *An Essay on the "Vita Nuova"* (Cambridge: Harvard University Press, 1949; reprint, Baltimore: Johns Hopkins University Press, 1977).

3. Domenico De Robertis, *Il libro della "Vita Nuova"* (Florence: Sansoni, 1961).

4. One of the main arguments advanced by De Robertis is that Dante's reading of Cicero's treatise on friendship (a *secular* treatise) was fundamental to his redefinition of love as an "eternal" bond. Regardless of the cogency of De Robertis's thesis, his overriding desire to establish continuity between Dante and the Latin tradition in this way is typically peninsular.

5. Giuseppe Mazzotta, "The Language of Poetry in the *Vita Nuova*," *Rivista di studi italiani* 1 (1983):3–14.

6. The trend starts with J. E. Shaw, *Essays on the "Vita Nuova"* (Princeton: Princeton University Press, 1929), and continues with Singleton's book, followed by Mark Musa's "An Essay on the *Vita Nuova*," in *Dante's "Vita Nuova,"* ed. and trans. Mark Musa (Bloomington: University of Indiana Press, 1973), and most recently by Jerome Mazzaro's *The Figure of Dante: An Essay on the "Vita Nuova"* (Princeton: Princeton University Press, 1981).

7. Barbara Nolan, a good example of a Singletonian critic, takes the revelocentric reading to an extreme by arguing for an analogy between the author of the *Vita Nuova* and the author of Revelation, each of whom "editorializes" his visions, so to speak. See "The *Vita Nuova*: Dante's Book of Revelation," *Dante Studies* 88 (1970):51–77.

8. Nicolò Mineo has convincingly argued that there is no rigorous or essential distinction between a *visione*, an *imaginazione*, and a

fantasia. See *Profetismo e Apocalittica in Dante* (Catania: Pubblicazioni della Facoltà di Lettere e Filosofia, 24, 1968), pp. 104ff.

9. It is not known when Dante began to read St. Bernard, but Edmund G. Gardner thinks that it was later in Dante's life; see *Dante and the Mystics* (New York: Haskell House, 1968), pp. 111ff.

1 Dante's Dream

1. It is difficult to determine the difference in status between Dante's actual "perceptions" of Beatrice in the *Vita Nuova* and his various dreams, visions, and hallucinations. Dante's perception of her in the street walking between two women has essentially the same visionary character as the dream to which the perception gives rise: she drifts by in white like an apparition, a vision. Hence the "marvelous vision" is more like a magnification of, or sequel to, the previous perception of Beatrice on the street. Robert Hollander discusses different modes of perception in the *Vita Nuova* in "*Vita Nuova*: Dante's Perceptions of Beatrice," *Dante Studies* 92 (1974):1–18. On the relation between "reality" and "imagination" in the *Vita Nuova*, see Pino da Prati, *Realtà e allegoria nella "Vita nuova" di Dante* (Sanremo: Edizioni "Grafiche Bracco," 1963).

2. Maurice Valency thought that Dante's discovery and exploitation of the poetic motif of the lady's death was a decisive event in literary history, setting the trend for Petrarch and future Petrarchists. "In terms of the stilnovist conceit," he writes, "obviously the best thing a lady could do for her lover was to die" (*In Praise of Love* [New York: Macmillan, 1969], p. 251).

3. "Three visions foretell her death. At the time of their coming, no one, not even her lover to whom they came, understood the sad forecast which they so obscurely made. But later, of course, after her death, anyone might see what their true meaning had been" (Singleton, *Essay*, p. 13). Even De Robertis accepts the general consensus: "[I]l presagio, come ormai generalmente s'intende, concerneva la morte di Beatrice" (*Il libro*, p. 39).

4. For both Cino da Pistoia's and Dante da Maiano's responses to Dante, see *Vita Nuova-Rime*, ed. Fredi Chiappelli (Milan: Mursia, 1973), pp. 79–80.

5. See my discussion in chapter 4.

6. The point was made by Rachel Jacoff in "The Poetry of Guido Cavalcanti" (Ph.D. diss., Yale University, 1979), pp. 127–28.

7. Guido's response to Dante (*Rime*, xxxviib) reads as follows:

Vedeste, al mio parere, onne valore
e tutto gioco e quanto bene om sente,
se foste in prova del segnor valente
che segnoreggia il mondo de l'onore,

poi vive in parte dove noia more,
e tien ragione nel casser de la mente;
si va soave per sonno a la gente,
che 'l core ne porta senza far dolore.

Di voi lo core portò, veggendo
che vostra donna alla morte cadea:
nodriala dello cor, di ciò temendo.

Quando v'apparve che se 'n gia dolendo,
fu 'l dolce sonno ch'allor si compiea,
ché 'l su' contraro lo venìa vincendo.

8. Dante's metaphorical use of the verb *vedere* follows Cavalcanti's systematic use of it in the cognitive sense. Thomas Aquinas thematizes the analogical relation between sensible and cognitive vision in the *Summa Theologiae* (henceforth *ST*): "Sicut patet in nomine visionis, quod primo impositum est ad significandum actum sensus visus; sed propter dignitatem et certitudinem huius sensus, extensum est hoc nomen, secundum usum locquentium, ad omnem cognitionem aliorum sensuum . . . et ulterius etiam ad cognitionem intellectus" (*ST*1 qu67 ar1 co).

9. Margherita de Bonfils Templer provides a survey of the diverse interpretations of the "marvelous vision" in her monograph *Itinerario di Amore: Dialettica di Amore e Morte nella "Vita Nuova,"* University of North Carolina Studies in Romance Languages and Literature (Chapel Hill, 1973), pp. 30–31.

10. White symbolizes faith; red stands for *caritas* (the etymon *car* occurs also in English words like *cardinal, carnation, carnal*—all of which are linked to the color red). The color green, which would complete the color symbolism of the theological virtues and give us the magical number three, is absent from the *Vita Nuova* (a note for Singletonians). Mark Musa discusses the color symbolism of Beatrice's appearances in "Essay on the *Vita Nuova*," pp. 102–3.

11. Gayatri Chakravorty Spivak calls it a "wet dream" and offers

a feminist reading that tells us more about psychoanalytic hermeneutics than about the *Vita Nuova*. She finds in the vision an archetypical "transfer of responsibility" in Dante's adoption of the "passive" role with regard both to Beatrice, who has eaten the heart, and to the lord, who forced her to eat it: "Beatrice, then, is said to *make* Dante act so. . . . By being an object who apparently regulates the subject's action, she allows the subject to deconstruct its sovereign motive and to disguise its masochism/narcissism" ("Finding Feminist Readings: Dante-Yeats," *Social Text* 2 [Fall 1980]:19).

12. For the traditional status of the lord see Thomas Hyde's recent book, *The Poetic Theology of Love: Cupid in the Renaissance* (Newark: University of Delaware Press, 1986), esp. pp. 45–72.

13. The consumption of the burning heart has provoked numerous interpretations, some of them as bizarre as the oneiric event itself. Many of them fasten upon the theme of nourishment and propose that love is being nourished by the consumption; but the love is Dante's and not Beatrice's, hence it is difficult to follow the logic of this argument. Barbara Nolan has suggested that the scene alludes to St. John's eating of the book offered by the angel in Rev. 10:8–11 ("*Vita Nuova*: Dante's Book of Revelation"). More recently she has suggested that "Beatrice as Christ draws the narrator's burning heart into herself. She accepts his all-too-human courtly love (hence her distaste) by eating his heart . . . at the hand of her Lord, Love" (see "The *Vita Nuova* and Richard of St. Victor's Phenomenology of Vision," *Dante Studies* 92 [1974]:44). Let's repeat that: Christ accepts Dante's courtly love at the hand of *her Lord, Love*?

Mark Musa attempts to distinguish between the so-called Greater Aspect and the Lesser Aspect of the lord and to argue that the gruesome act of forcing Beatrice to eat the heart belongs to the Lesser Aspect of this contradictory, protean figure ("Essay on the *Vita Nuova*," pp. 120–21). And so on.

The scene of the consumption would seem to cry out for a psychoanalytic reading. Spivak's assessment:

> If I decide to describe the events of this dream-vision through psychoanalytic structures, I can treat it as telling the story of a fantasy where the woman allows the man to acquire a "passivity" that would prohibit "activity." By devouring Dante's phallus—the bleeding heart is a thin disguise—Beatrice "incorporates" him, "identifies" with him, acts for

NOTES TO PAGES 25–27 175

him. . . . Now that Beatrice has been unwillingly made to introject, Dante can . . . inaugurate a war against this integrated female (she's filled with the phallus now, after all). The war is also a self-glorification since it is his own phallus. . . . The woman's desire is nowhere in question, she remains mute, acts against her will, and possesses the phallus by a grotesque transplant. ("Finding Feminist Readings," p.18) The "transplant" in this instance seems that of psychoanalysis into the dream, with its attendant reading of the *Vita Nuova* as a war against the "integrated female." Another transplant is that of the "bleeding heart." While the image occurs in Yeats, the heart in Dante's dream is a flaming, not a bleeding, one ("una cosa la quale ardesse tutta").

14. Marianne Shapiro undertakes an extended analysis of the role of metonymy in the *Vita Nuova* and affirms that the lord is invariably metonymic in his rhetorical status. In her long discussion of the dream, however, she fails to point out that the burning heart represents a metonymic emblem of the narrator himself; see "Figurality in the *Vita Nuova*: Dante's New Rhetoric," *Dante Studies* 97 (1979):107–27.

15. See Giuseppe Mazzotta's discussion of the traditional motif of the eaten heart in his analysis of Boccaccio's tale of Ghismunda: *The World at Play in Boccaccio's "Decameron"* (Princeton: Princeton University Press, 1986), pp. 131–58.

16. In a note on the dream in his annotated edition, *Vita Nuova-Rime*, Chiappelli writes: "Torna forse qui il rammentare che Bice Portinari andò sposa giovanissima, e che la sua condizione di maritata dové pure influire sulle reazioni del giovane. La drammaticità di questa . . . considerazione . . . si riconosce in molti particolari della visione" (pp. 21–22).

17. Margherita de Bonfils Templer's thesis that the scene depicts love outside of the sober control of the "consiglio de la ragione," and therefore figures as an affirmation of love as *passion*, is well sustained, but the idea that the consumption signifies the transgressive act of physical union is a conclusion that directly contradicts the refiguration or redimensionalization of passion which takes place in the vision; see "Amore e le visioni nella *Vita Nuova*," *Dante Studies* 92 (1974):24.

18. In the Ottimo's gloss on the word *sanguigno* in *Inferno* v, we read: "Pone tutto per parte: sicche questo sanguigno denomina il sangue, cioè il colore cardinalesco che noi chiamiamo sanguigno" (*L'Ot-*

timo commento della Divinia Commedia, ed. A. Torri, 3 vols. [Pisa: Niccolò Capurro, 1927–29] 1:84).

19. The moment of Beatrice's appearance in *Purgatory* xxx is fraught with recalls to the early work. As Rachel Jacoff notes in her essay "*Purgatorio* xxx" (forthcoming in *Lectura Dantis Californiana* [Berkeley and Los Angeles: University of California Press]), "The linkages between the *Vita Nuova* and the *Commedia* are nowhere more visible than in this canto where even the title of the earlier work makes its way into the text (at v.115)." Surely, then, it is no accident that a phenomenology of veils and dress pervades Dante's description of this first imaginary reappearance of Beatrice after so many years: "sovra candido vel cinta d'uliva / donna m'apparve, sotto verde manto / vestita di color di fiamma viva" (ll. 31–33).

20. I do not employ the terms *phenomenal* and *noumenal* in a strict Kantian sense, though they are loosely related to Kant's dichotomy between the thing in itself and its appearance to perception. In *Kant and the Problem of Metaphysics*, trans. James S. Churchill (Bloomington: University of Indiana Press, 1962), Heidegger remarks that the noumenon is merely God's totalized view of an entity (p. 36). As suggested by the presence of the veil, such noumenal vision is denied to Dante in his dream; however, in the last chapter of the *libello* Dante speaks of a "miraculous vision" of Beatrice in heaven which alludes to a noumenal vision in Heidegger's sense.

2 The Ideal Lyric

1. For a comprehensive analysis of the Bonagiunta passage and its interpretations in the history of the scholarship, see Theodolinda Barolini, *Dante's Poets: Textuality and Truth in the "Comedy"* (Princeton: Princeton University Press, 1984), pp. 85–123; see also Marcello Ciccuto, "Dante e Bonagiunta: reperti allusivi nel canto xxiv del *Purgatorio*," *Lettere italiane* (1982):386–395.

2. Classic studies of stilnovism include: Mario Marti, *Storia dello stil novo* (Lecce: Milella, 1973); Ernesto Savona, *Repertorio tematico del dolce stil novo* (Bari: Adriatica, 1973); Giorgio Petrocchi, "Il Dolce stil novo," in *Storia della letterature italiana*, ed. Emilio Cecchi (Milano: Garzanti, 1965), pp. 727–74; Gianfranco Contini, *Poeti del Duecento*, vol. 2 (Milano-Napoli: Riccardi, 1960); Guido Favati, *Inchiesta sul Dolce*

Stil Nuovo (Firenze: Le Monnier, 1975); Antonio Enzo Quaglio, *Lo stilnovo e la poesia religiosa* (Bari: Laterza, 1971); Emilio Bigi, "Genesi di un concetto storiografico," *Giornale storico della letterature italiana* 132 (1955):333–71. For an exhaustive bibliography of the studies of Guinizelli's innovational role for stilnovism see Vincent Moleta, *Guinizelli in Dante* (Roma: Edizioni di storia e letteratura, 1980), p. 11. Both Contini and Favati, and to some extent De Robertis, believe that if there actually existed a school of stilnovist poets, Guido Cavalcanti was its sole leader and inspiration. Favati goes so far as to deny that the stilnovists formed either a group of poets or a group of friends and argues that Cavalcanti was the single *maestro* towering over the other poets who were associated or connected with him. Other critics, for example Mark Musa, reject the notion of stilnovism altogether (see Musa's *Advent at the Gates: Dante's Comedy* [Bloomington: Indiana University Press, 1974], pp. 111–28). I share Barolini's sober view that "(1) there is a new style that pertains to a group of new poets . . . (2) within this new style, there is a truly new style, characterized by the *nove rime*, and this is Dante's own *stil novo*" (*Dante's Poets*, p. 86n). The purpose of the present chapter is to uncover the essence of the new style within stilnovism.

3. See Maurice Valency's assessment of stilnovism in relation to the Provençal tradition in *In Praise of Love*, pp. 205–55. See also Fredric Goldin's account of the intellectualization of love poetry among the stilnovists as an attempt to reconstitute elitist courtly bonds in the absence of the Provençal court setting: *German and Italian Lyrics of the Middle Ages: An Anthology and a History*, trans. and ed. by Fredric Goldin (Garden City, N.Y.: Anchor Books, 1973), pp. 343–63.

4. For Bonagiunta's sonnet to Guinizelli and Guinizelli's response to Bonagiunta, see Contini, *Poeti del Duecento*, 2:481–82.

5. Note: this single *active* gesture of Beatrice in *Vita Nuova* x— prompted by jealousy, disdain, or misunderstanding—redeems her otherwise passive role in the narrative action.

6. A compelling critical analysis of the epideictic convention in medieval and Renaissance poetry is provided thoughout Joel Fineman's recent book *Shakespeare's Perjured Eye: The Invention of Poetic Subjectivity in the Sonnets* (Berkeley and Los Angeles: University of California Press, 1986); see especially the Introduction (pp. 1–48) for a discussion of the broad historical parameters of the lyric of praise. Fineman also believes that Dante's decision in the *Vita Nuova* to write only

poems of praise remains a momentous one for literary history: "As early as Dante's *La Vita Nuova*, for example, in a passage that Dante will later remember as inaugurating the *Dolce stil nuovo*, the 'beatitude' (*beatitudine*) of the poet, which is to say 'the goal of [his] desire,' is not only expressed by, but is explicitly identified with, 'those words that praise my lady' (*In quelle parole che lodano la donna mia*)" (p. 49). Scattered quotations from Fineman's book reveal the degree to which Dante's turn toward epideixis is posited at the origin of a long subsequent lyric tradition: "This is a central fact for the Renaissance sonnet, which, from Dante onward, characteristically presents itself as something panegyric" (p. 1); "The poetry of praise, that is to say, especially in the sonneteering tradition that begins with Dante" (p. 134); "As the sonnet evolves from Dante to Shakespeare there is a transition from an epideictic ontology to an epideictic psychology" (p. 217); "It is as though homosexuality were the secret truth of all ideal and idealizing desire from Dante onwards" (p. 256).

7. See Kierkegaard's "Eulogy of Abraham" in *Fear and Trembling*, trans. and ed. Howard V. Hong and Edna H. Hong (Princeton: Princeton University Press, 1983), pp. 15–16.

8. The verse comes from Hölderlin's poem "Rememberance." For the English translation of Hölderlin's complete poems see *Friedrich Hölderlin: Poems and Fragments*, trans. Michael Hamburger (Ann Arbor: University of Michigan Press, 1967). For a ponderous but far-reaching ontological interpretation of the verse, see Martin Heidegger's essay "Hölderlin and the Essence of Poetry," in *Existence and Being*, ed. Werner Brock (Chicago: Gateway, 1949), pp. 270–91, esp. pp. 280–82.

9. I am grateful to Professor Anthony Brophy from the Overseas School of Rome for opening up this perspective on Pindar's poetics for me.

10. Fineman, *Shakespeare's Perjured Eye*, p. 6.

11. De Robertis argues for the presence of a number of scriptural subtexts for chapters XVIII and XIX, which recount Dante's turn to the epideictic manner: "Preso a sé, il tema della lode beatificante, della lode come gioia, è tema scritturale, ed ha il suo centro di irradiazione nel libro dei *Salmi*" (*Il libro*, p. 104). Singleton also argues that the passage in chapter XVIII echoes the scriptural moment when Jesus answers Martha's complaint that her sister Mary sits at His feet while she does the housework (Luke 10:41–42): "In view of the analogy between the

contemplative life (for which Mary stood) and the contemplative nature of the second stage of love in the *Vita Nuova*, I venture to suggest that such an echo is not illusory and that it, too, helps to say why the second stage is more noble than the first" (*Essay*, p. 153). De Robertis claims that the echo pointed out by Singleton is "indubitable" (*Il libro*, p. 101).

12. The subtle pattern of reflection is analyzed and emphasized by Vittorio Russo, "Il 'nodo' del Dolce Stil Novo," *Medioevo romanzo* 39 (1976):236-64. Russo claims that Dante's new style is the "fruit of an artistic maturity" Dante reached after being under the tutelage of the Sicilian School, the Provençal tradition, and the "maniera dotta" of the Tuscan School. Eduardo Sanguineti also insists on demystifying the notion of mere "inspiration" and emphasizes the role of reflection in Dante's turn to a new manner ("Per una lettura della *Vita Nuova*," preface to *Dante: Vita Nuova* [Milano: Garzanti, 1983], pp. xxxii-xxxiii). For a more extended discussion along similar lines, see Francesco Tateo, "La 'nuova matera' e la svolta critica della *Vita Nuova*," in *Studi di filologia romanza offerti a Silvio Pellegrini* (Padova: Liviana, 1971), pp. 629-53.

13. Giorgio Barberi Squarotti remarks that what is also at issue in the breakthrough is Dante's ennoblement of vernacular verse by virtue of its address to women, who, as Dante explains in chapter xxv, were the original addressees of the first vernacular love poems; see "Introduzione alla *Vita Nuova*," in *Opere Minori di Dante Alighieri*, 2 vols. (Torino: UTET, 1983), 1:30-32.

14. Aquinas's highly succinct formula reads: "Integritas sive perfectio, debita proportio sive consonantia, et iterum claritas" (*ST*1 qu39 ar8 co). Integrity or perfection is to be understood ontologically as actualized existence, or the act whereby an essence stands outside of its causes and is opposed to non-being (Beatrice as salvific). Proportion or harmony is to be understood not so much as symmetry but as the conformity of parts with the intrinsic end that is determined by a thing's form (Beatrice as the exemplum of beauty: "che Dio ne 'ntendea di far cosa nova," v. 46). Clarity is to be understood as the intelligible radiance of form that pervades a being (Beatrice as "maraviglia ne l'atto che procede / d'un'anima che 'nfin qua su risplende," vv. 16-17). Dante's *canzone*, however, emphasizes above all Beatrice's luminosity, hence I will be dealing more with the dimension of *claritas* in the following pages.

15. Aquinas did not compose any special treatise on aesthetics, precisely because he considered beauty not merely a privileged category of the fine arts but a transcendental common to all entities: "Nihil est quod non participet pulchro et bono" (*In Dionysii de Divinis Nominibus*: cp4 1c5 260). Like the other transcendentals, beauty occurs analogically or proportionately in created things. What is essential for a Thomistic aesthetics is that beauty is in every case embodied. For a fine analysis of Aquinas's aesthetic theories, see Umberto Eco's doctoral dissertation, *Il problema estetico in Tommaso d'Aquino* (published by Edizioni di "Filosofia" [Torino, 1954], reprinted by Bompiani [Milano, 1970]). For a more rudimentary treatment see Thomas Gilby, *Poetic Experience: An Introduction to Thomist Aesthetics* (New York: Russel and Russel, 1934).

16. "Forma autem a qua dependet propria ratio rei, pertinet ad claritatem" (*In Dionysii de Divinis Nominibus*: cp4 1c6 160).

17. "Intellectus noster non est proportionatus ad cognoscendum naturali cognitione aliquid nisi per sensibilia" (*In Libros Sententiarium*: I ds3 qu1 ra2).

18. I take the word *emotion* in an almost literal sense here as that which *moves*. In Dante's case it is the e-motion of the poetic tongue: "la mia lingua parlò quasi come per se stessa *mossa*."

19. *ST1* qu5 ar4 ra1. Also "Pulchrum autem dicatur id cuius ipsa apprehensio placet" (*ST2* qu27 ar1 ra3).

20. *ST2* qu27 ar1 ra3. In this passage of the *Summa Theologiae*, Aquinas discusses the relation between the good and the beautiful, stating that they are akin insofar as both placate the turbulence of appetition; they are different, however, in the manner by which each brings about this placation (*pulchrum est idem bono, sola ratione differens*). The good functions as a "final cause" of desire, and the appetite is placated when it takes possession of the good by direct acquisition; the beautiful, on the other hand, engages the *cognitive* power (*Pulchra autem respicit vim cognoscitivam*). As a "formal cause" (*pulchrum proprie pertinet ad rationem causae formalis*), beauty placates by being seen, that is to say, by being apprehended. It brings repose to the appetite not by being directly possessed but rather by being contemplated for its own sake. In short, the "pleasure" of the beautiful is linked to that category of "disinterested reflection" which seems to be the keystone of much later aesthetic theories, Immanuel Kant's, for example.

21. "Pulchrum autem respicit vim cognoscitvam, pulchra enim dicuntur quae visa placent" (*ST*1 qu5 ar4 ra1).

22. James Joyce, *Portrait of the Artist as a Young Man* (New York: Viking Press, 1971), p. 213.

23. "There is in the sonnet a process of internalization as it moves from the evocation of the outside world . . . into the heart of the beholder, to the moment when the spirit tells the soul to sigh" (Mazzotta, "Language of Poetry in the *Vita Nuova*," p. 11). See also R. L. Martinez's remarks in "The Pilgrim's Answer to Bonagiunta and the Poetics of the Spirit," *Stanford Italian Review* 3 (1983):37–63. Bernard S. Levy, quoting from the gospel of John (20:19–20), argues that "the concatenation of images suggests that Dante had in mind as analogue the scene following Christ's Resurrection in which Christ breathes the Holy Spirit—the Spirit of Love—upon his disciples" ("Beatrice's Greeting and Dante's 'Sigh' in the *Vita Nuova*," *Dante Studies* 92 [1974]:59).

24. Joyce, *Portrait*, p. 206. Clearly the phenomenon of rhythm is the most elusive element in the aesthetic emotion. I am tempted to say that the "rhythm of beauty" is in some sense the body of Beatrice itself. In any case, nowhere in his extended discussion of poetic composition and prosaic decomposition does Dante account for the element of rhythm. Like the rhythm of Beatrice's passage, the rhythms of poetry are wholly intangible, even after a meticulous breaking up of the poem into parts. " 'What is that exactly?' asked Lynch [about the rhythm of beauty]. 'Rhythm,' said Stephen, 'is the first formal esthetic relation of part to part in any esthetic whole or of an esthetic whole to its part or parts or of any part to the esthetic whole of which it is a part' " (p. 206). The Scholastics defined the body as "parts outside of parts." This is the sort of rhythm which the *divisioni*, however elaborately they break a poem into parts, will never lay bare.

3 Figures of Love

1. In his essay "*Vita Nuova*: Dante's Perceptions of Beatrice," Robert Hollander finds it strange that "in view of Dante's fondness for the number [nine]," no Dante scholar has attempted to count the number of times Beatrice appears to Dante in the *Vita Nuova*. I find it strange that no Dante scholar has asked what the number logically implies with regard to Beatrice. The number nine is above all a *tempo-*

ral measure. It marks dates, hours, years; it marks the limits within which an event takes place. It refers, therefore, to a principle of temporal containment, and hence, by extension, to the finitude of Beatrice. Its recurrence constitutes a promise of continuity within the finite limits of time. It is this promise that the narrative as a whole incorporates and makes its own *as a promise*. It is perhaps even this promise that ends the narrative in xlii.

2. Both poems were composed years before Dante wrote the *Vita Nuova*, but according to Michele Barbi, the sonnet was written at the same time as "Donne ch'avete," namely in 1289 (*Problemi di critica dantesca*, 2 vols. [Florence: Sansoni, 1975], 1:104). Patrick Boyde believes that it could have been composed earlier, around 1287 (*Dante's Style in His Lyric Poetry* [Cambridge: Cambridge University Press, 1971], p. 348). In the *Vita Nuova*, however, Dante claims that he had already achieved a certain notoriety for "Donne ch'avete" before composing it.

3. My use of the term *person* deliberately evokes its specific theological significance in Scholastic philosophy, where the discussion centers around the categories of substance and accident invoked by Dante in chapter xxv. One of the earliest formulations of the concept as it was later understood by the Scholastic tradition is provided by Boethius in his *De Persona et Duabas Naturis*, which defines person as "an individual substance of a rational nature" (Minge PL 64, col.1345). Boethius's use of the term *substance* is Aristotelian and refers to "first substance" (*prote ousia*) in Aristotle's sense of the radically singular and particular thing ("Substance in the truest and primary sense of the word is that which is neither predicable of a subject nor present in a subject, for instance the individual man or horse" [*Categories* 2a, 12]). Thomas Aquinas accepted Boethius's definition but extended it to mean a substance that is complete, subsists by itself, and is separated from others. Translated into terms that mean something for us: the person of Beatrice remains singular and substantial and unthinkable apart from her body, since the body is that which, for the Scholastics, individuates and singularizes a person.

4. Eduardo Sanguineti claims that the poet's bedroom is the privileged interior space of the lyric venture: "Così la 'camera' del poeta, come 'solingo luogo' si impone subito quale centro ideale dell'intera avventura lirica della *Vita nuova*" ("Per una lettura della *Vita Nuova*," p. xxi). I believe that while Sanguineti is generally correct

with regard to the first half of Dante's *libello*, there is clearly a change in orientation—from private to public space—toward the middle of the narrative.

5. Giorgio Agamben, *Infanzia e storia* (Torino: Einaudi, 1983), p. 18 [my translation].

6. On the question of reification, Agamben indicts Boccaccio for committing one of the great blunders in literary history when he identified Dante's Beatrice with a certain Beatrice di Portinari of Florence. Because of Boccaccio, says Agamben, we have since missed the point: that Beatrice was not a woman at all but a phantasm belonging to the imagination. While there is a degree of reification in attempting to identify the "real" woman behind the poetry, it is likewise essential to Dante's vision of Beatrice that she *is* a woman and not merely a phantasm of the imagination. See Agamben, "Il Sogno della Lingua: Per una lettura di Polifilo," *Lettere italiane* 4 (1982):478–79.

7. Sanguineti, "Per una lettura della *Vita Nuova*," p. xvii [my translation].

8. On Dante's theory of the genealogy of vernacular composition, see Ettore Paratore's *Tradizione e struttura in Dante* (Florence: Sansoni, 1968), pp. 25–121. More generally see E. R. Curtius, "Dante und das lateinische Mittelalter," *Neue Dantestudien* 60 (1947):281–89. In relation to the *Vita Nuova* in particular, see Charles S. Singleton, "The Use of Latin in the *Vita Nuova*," *Modern Language Notes* 30 (1946):108–12. For an encyclopedic study of the relation between Latin and Italian vernacular poetry, see vol. 1 of Peter Dronke's *Medieval Latin and the Rise of European Love-Lyric*, 2d ed., 2 vols. (Oxford: Clarendon Press, 1968).

9. Michelangelo Picone dicusses the relationship between figures of speech and *ragione* in *"Vita Nuova" e tradizione romanza* (Padova: Liviana Editrice, 1979), pp. 18–26.

10. See Francesco Tateo's analysis of the critical "responsibility" of the vernacular poet in " 'Aprire per prosa': Le premesse critiche della poetica dantesca," in *Studi in onore di Antonio Corsano* (Manduria: Lacaita, 1970), pp. 31–64. See also Ignazio Baldelli, "Sul rapporto fra prosa e poesia nella *Vita Nuova*," *Rassegna della letteratura italiana* 80 (1976):325–37.

11. The irony is stongest perhaps in Dante's famous poem to Cavalcanti, "Guido i' vorrei," which imagines Cavalcanti, Lapo Gianni, and Dante, along with their ladies, on an enchanted ship sail-

ing the seas. Dante's velleity consists of *discoursing on love* with his fellow poets, perhaps on deck. It is not clear what the women on board would be doing while the men talked.

12. Elaborating the four levels of interpretation in *Convivio*, ii. 1.4, Dante distinguishes the literal from the allegorical meaning of a poem in terms that are eloquent with associations for us by now: "One is called literal, because it does not extend beyond the letter of the fictitious words, as in the case of the fables of the poets. The other is called allegorical, because it is that which hides under the cloak [*manto*] of these fables, and is a truth hidden beneath a beautiful lie."

13. Cf. John Freccero, "Infernal Irony: The Gates of Hell," in *Dante's Poetics of Conversion*, ed. Rachel Jacoff (Cambridge: Harvard University Press, 1986), pp. 93–110; also idem, "Medusa: The Letter and the Spirit" (pp. 119–136).

14. Some scholars have tried to read the *Vita Nuova* as a rigorous and extended allegory, and the results are somewhat astonishing. In two of the most explicit cases of allegorical interpretation—those of Philippe Guibertereau and Gertrude Leigh—the scholars find in Dante's relationship to Beatrice an allegory of his relation to the Church. The hermeneutic virtuosity of Leigh's book, *The Passing of Beatrice: A Study in the Heterodoxy of Dante* (London: Faber and Faber, 1932), is equal to its sheer philological rigor, expressed for example by the following piece of (mis)information in the introduction: "Dissatisfied with the meaning assigned to the *New Life* by many, and more particularly perturbed by the gross interpretation of his emotional narrative accepted by some, Dante set himself a few years later to write an explanation of the Odes [*sic*] contained in it. He called this work *The Banquet* (p. ix). Guibertereau's study (*L'enigme de Dante* [Paris: Deseclée de Brouwer, 1973]) is more sober, but he is not more persuasive when he interprets the episode of the screen lady in chapter v of the *Vita Nuova* as the allegory of Dante's moral deviance from the Church, allegorized in Beatrice. A more thoughtful discussion of allegory from the point of view of the difference between vision and actuality in the narrative of the *Vita Nuova* is provided by see Pino da Prati, *Realtà e allegoria nella "Vita Nuova" di Dante*.

15. On the relationship between poetry and prose in general in the *Vita Nuova*, see Aldo Vallone, *La prosa della "Vita Nuova"* (Firenze: Le Monnier, 1963), esp. pp. 40–56. See also De Robertis's "L'idea del libro," in *Il libro*, pp. 5–24. See also M. Picone, "Strutture

poetiche e strutture prosastiche nella *Vita Nuova*," *Modern Language Notes* 92 (1977):117–29. Ignazio Baldelli discusses chapter xxv's articulation of the poetry/prose question in "Sul rapporto fra prosa e poesia nella *Vita Nuova*."

16. In *Dante's Lyric Poetry* (Oxford: Clarendon Press, 1967), Foster and Boyde document every instance in the *Vita Nuova* where the author strips the "garment" of figurative speech (see under "vesta di figura" in the index). With the sole exception of a personification of the poet's eyes as "due disiri" in the sonnet "Lasso, per forza di molti sospiri," it is the figure of love which in each case is the "vesta di figura" removed by the author.

17. Pio Rajna was the first to associate the *divisioni* with the Scholastic exegetical practice of dividing the text. He showed, for example, the correspondence between terms like *ibi* in the Scholastic protocol and *quivi* in Dante's prose. Rajna argued that Dante's ceremonious divisions put the author in the role of a schoolman in a classroom and the reader in the position of a schoolboy quite literally "listening" to the master's lecture (Dante actually uses the word *udire* in the division of "Donne ch'avete" to refer to the reader's "getting the message" about the meaning of the poem). For Rajna's study, see "Per le 'divisioni' della 'Vita Nuova,' " *Strenna Dantesca* 1 (1902):111–14. Panofsky, in his book *Gothic Architecture and Scholasticism* (Latrobe: Archabbey Press, 1951), finds that Dante's breaking down of a *canzone* into parts and parts of parts embodies or instantiates the essential link between Gothic architectural practices and Scholastic argumentation, both of which depend on a "sufficent articulation" of parts in the system's totality. But do Dante's *divisioni* really accomplish something in this respect? "I wonder," asks Musa, "if [Dante] might not have had an artistic interest [as opposed to a hermeneutic one] in breaking down a poetic structure into conceptual units." I cannot see what artistic purpose the *divisioni* could have, but I am in accord with Musa that "there are few interpretations, allegorical or otherwise, contained in the *divisioni* of the *Vita Nuova*" ("Essay on the *Vita Nuova*," p. 96). For an extended discussion of the role of the *divisioni* for the "architecture" of the *Vita Nuova* in its relation to both Scholastic argumentation and Gothic constructive practices, see Jerome Mazzaro, *The Figure of Dante: An Essay on the "Vita Nuova"* (Princeton: Princeton University Press, 1981), pp. 51–70.

18. Northop Frye's remark comes from *The Anatomy of Criticism*

(Princeton: Princeton University Press, 1957), p. 249. It recalls of course T. S. Eliot's declaration that in first-person poetry the poet expresses "his own thoughts and sentiments to himself or to no one." For further discussion, see Lewis Freed, *T. S. Eliot: The Critic as Philosopher* (Lafayette, Ind.: Purdue University Press, 1979), pp. 174–80.

19. Paul de Man's figural reading of the lyric is found throughout his essays on Romanticism. Some of the more explicit elaborations of his theory are in the essays "Anthropomorphism and Trope in the Lyric," in *The Rhetoric of Romanticism* (New York: Columbia University Press, 1984), pp. 239–62, and "Lyrical Voice in Contemporary Theory," in *Lyric Poetry: Beyond New Criticism*, ed., Chaviva Hošek and Patricia Parker (Ithaca, N.Y.: Cornell University Press, 1985), pp. 55–72; Jonathan Culler's overview of post-new-critical interpretations of the lyric is presented in his essay "Changes in the Study of the Lyric," in *Lyric Poetry: Beyond New Criticism*, pp. 38–54; see also *The Pursuit of Signs* (Ithaca, N.Y.: Cornell University Press, 1981), pp. 135–54.

20. De Man, "Lyrical Voice in Contemporary Theory," p. 61.

21. The problem of poetic description versus figural inscription is the issue of a debate between Paul de Man and Michel Riffaterre. See de Man, "Hypogram and Inscription: Michel Riffaterre's Poetics of Reading," *Diacritics* xi (Winter 1981):19–29. For Riffaterre's response to de Man's critique, see "Prosopopoeia," in *Lessons of Paul de Man*, ed. Peter Brooks, Shoshana Felman, and J. Hillis Miller, Yale French Studies no. 69 (New Haven: Yale University Press, 1986), pp. 107–23.

22. Cf. Barbara Johnson, "Apostrophe, Animation, and Abortion," *Diacritics* 16 (Spring 1986):29–39.

23. The title of Cynthia Chase's recent book, *Decomposing Figures* (Baltimore: Johns Hopkins University Press, 1986), which presents rhetorical readings in the romantic tradition from the figuralist perspective, could well serve as the rubric for Dante's digression in xxv. In her introduction (p. 6), Chase declares that the peculiar feature of Romantic poetry is its "heightened sense" of the instabilities of figurative language. Without denying the claim, I would say that medieval Italian lyricists like Cavalcanti, Dante, and Petrarch were as consciously and explicitly preoccupied with these instabilities as any in literary history. In any case it is almost impossible to read a poem by Guido Cavalcanti and not find an ontology of figures at its very center.

4 The Ghost of Guido Cavalcanti

1. For a classic introduction to the stylistic innovations of Cavalcanti, see Guido Favati, "Tecnica ed arte nella poesia cavalcantiana," *Studi petrarchesi* 3 (1950):117–41. To Favati, who devoted a lifetime to Cavalcanti's poetry, we owe the superb critical edition of the *Rime* (Milan: Ricciardi, 1957). See also Maria Corti's early article "La fisionomia stilistica di Guido Cavalcanti," in *Rendiconti dell'Accademia dei Lincei*, series 8, vol. 5 (1950), pp. 530–52.

2. One of the finest treatments of this phantasmology is Giorgio Agamben's *Stanze: La parola e il fantasma nella cultura occidentale* (Torino: Einaudi, 1977), pp. 105–29. Agamben's contribution in this domain is much indebted to the reconstructive work of Robert Klein in his seminal essay "Spirito Peregrino," *Revue d'etudes Italiennes* xi (1965):197–236; reprinted in *La forme et l'intelligible* (Paris: Gallimard, 1970), pp. 31–64.

3. Gianfranco Contini (*Poeti del Duecento*, 2:495) points to an allusion in *Canticum canticorum*: "Quae est ista quae progreditur?" (6:9). Though the strategy is found far less frequently in Cavalcanti, De Robertis finds here the literary precedent for Dante's systematic engagement with scriptural allusion (*Il libro*, pp. 44–45).

4. Corrado Calenda analyzes the role of the interrogative in Cavalcanti's corpus and documents every instance of it throughout the *Rime*. The frequency is startling. See *Per altezza d'ingegno: Saggio su Guido Cavalcanti* (Naples: Liguori, 1976), pp. 27–30.

5. Ezra Pound thought Cavalcanti was one of the subtlest poets of all times, but he emphasized his "radiant intellect" rather than the dark despair. Pound actually saw a deep link between "Donna me prega," a poem of darkness, and *De Luce*, believing that the *canzone* names the source of all light as love. Perhaps it's a deliberate misreading. Pound of course translated Cavalcanti's *Rime* and alludes to Guido some twenty times in the *Cantos*. In the majority of cases, these allusions recall Guido's descriptions of light. As Rachel Jacoff notes, "Pound, whose favorite dictum was Erigena's 'Omnia quae sunt, lumina sunt,' had to re-write Cavalcanti in order to appropriate him" ("Poetry of Guido Cavalcanti," p. 170). For Pound's views on Cavalcanti see his essay "Cavalcanti" in *The Literary Essays of Ezra Pound*, ed. T. S. Eliot (Norfolk: New Directions, 1954), pp. 149–200.

6. The term *tragic style* is used by Fredric Goldin, among others,

in what remains one of the best introductions to Cavalcanti's poetry in English, along with Lowry Nelson's; see *German and Italian Lyrics of the Middle Ages*, pp. 298–311. For Lowry Nelson's introduction see *The Poetry of Guido Cavalcanti*, ed. and trans. Lowry Nelson (New York: Garland Publishing, 1986). The English translations of Guido's poetry in this chapter come from this bilingual edition of the complete poems. With the publication of this fine edition there is no longer any reason why an English-speaking lover of poetry should remain ignorant of Cavalcanti's achievement in literary history.

7. The debate about Guido's Averroism is widespread but features Bruno Nardi and Guido Favati as the main antagonists. In "Noterella polemica sull'averroismo di Guido Cavalcanti," *Rassegna di filosofia* 3 (1954):47–71, Nardi attacked Favati's earlier view that Guido's philosophical concerns had been much exaggerated, and argued that Guido was a subtle and by no means naive Averroist. Favati responded with "Guido Cavalcanti, Dino del Garbo e l'avveroismo di Bruno Nardi," *Filologia romanza* 2 (1955):67–83. According to Favati's later reflection in his *Inchiesta sul Dolce Stil Nuovo*, Guido was an orthodox, not a radical, Aristotelian. Nardi's thesis about Guido's Avveroism is developed also in "L'averroismo del 'primo amico' di Dante" (*Dante e la cultura medievale*, ed. Paolo Mazzantini, 2d ed. rev. [Bari: Laterza, 1949], pp. 93–129). In a review of Ezra Pound's edition of the *Rime*, Etienne Gilson expresses skepticism about Guido's Averroism; see "Review of Guido Cavalcanti, *Rime*," *Criterion* 12 (1932–33):106–12. Other versions of Guido's philosophical leanings include J. E. Shaw's, who read him in terms of Albert the Great (*Guido Cavalcanti's Theory of Love* [Toronto: University of Toronto Press, 1949]), and Mario Casella's, who read him as a strict Thomist ("La canzone d'amore di Guido Cavalcanti," *Studi di filologia italiana* 7 [1942]:97–160). It is interesting to note that a year after Nardi's attack on Favati, Paul Oskar Kristeller's discovery and publication of an Averroist treatise dedicated to Guido lent considerable credence to Nardi's thesis ("A Philosophical Treatise from Bologna Dedicated to Guido Cavalcanti: Magister Jacobus de Pistorio and his 'Questio de Felicitate,' " included in *Medioevo e Rinascimento: Studi in onore di Bruno Nardi*, 2 vols. [Florence: Sansoni, 1955], 1:425–63). The treatise by Jacobus de Pistorio was recently exploited by Maria Corti to read "Donna me prega" in technical philosophical terms and to demonstrate, persuasively in my opinion, that Guido's *canzone* is wholly

Averroist in its doctrines. See *La felicità mentale: Nuove prospettive per Cavalcanti e Dante* (Torino: Einaudi, 1983); see also her discussion of Averroism in *Inferno* x in *Dante a un nuovo crocevia* (Florence: Sansoni, 1981), pp. 77–85.

8. In her gloss on vv. 21–23 of "Donna me prega" ("Vèn da veduta forma che s'intende, / Che prende—nel possible intelletto, / come in subieto,—loco e dimoranza"), Maria Corti points out that "according to radical Aristotelianism [i.e., Averroism] . . . the thinking *subject* is not the individual man, but is identified with the possible intellect or the separate and universal substance, which exploits the human body and sensitive soul as its *object*" (*La felicità mentale*, p. 23 [my translation]).

9. Calenda calls it the *vocabulorum discretio* and remarks that the "generic referentiality" of these words, which occur invariably in contexts of semantic indeterminacy, as pure evocations, is redeemed by a "unity of motivation" which determines their precise structural recurrence (*Per altezza d'ingegno*, p. 96). Michael P. Ginsburg has shown that while Cavalcanti's poetry is restricted on the semantic and lexical levels, it becomes highly inventive on the phonemic, syntactical, and metric levels; see "Literary Convention and Poetic Technique: The Poetry of Cavalcanti and Dante," *Italica* 4 (1977):485–501.

10. Guido's *canzone* has generated endless commentary, beginning with Dino del Garbo, who seems to have set the trend by approaching it more as a philosophical treatise than as a poem. In addition to the relevant essays and books cited in note 7, see Guido Favati, "La canzone d'amore del Cavalcanti," *Letteratura moderna* 3 (1952):18–32.; Bruno Nardi, "Di un nuovo commento alla canzone del Cavalcanti sull'amore," in *Dante e la cultura medievale*, pp. 130–52; Ferdinando Pappalardo, "Per una rilettura della canzone d'amore del Cavalcanti," *Studi e problemi di critica testuale* 13 (1976):18–32. For an English edition of Dino del Garbo's "Commentary," see Otto Bird, "The Canzone d'amore of Cavalcanti According to the Commentary of Dino del Garbo," *Medieval Studies* (Toronto) 2 (1940):150–203.

11. Rachel Jacoff is one of the few scholars who has tried to put the philosophical issues in brackets and read the poem poetically to see how and why it constitutes a great *poem*; see "Poetry of Guido Cavalcanti," pp. 98 ff.

12. Mario Marti, *Poeti del Dolce stil nuovo* (Florence: Le Monnier, 1969), p. 157. For a superb analysis and interpretation of the figure of

personification in Cavalcanti in terms of a psychic drama, see Calenda, *Per altezza d'ingegno*, pp. 17–24 and 90–98.

13. Calenda cites the various instances in which love speaks in the first person to point out that love not only invariably threatens the lover with death but at times actually kills the lover or the organs associated with the destructive passion (*Per altezza d'ingegno*, pp. 18–20).

14. For a detailed bibliography and an account of the history of Dante's attitudes toward his "primo amico" see Barolini, *Dante's Poets*, esp. pp. 123–52. See also Contini's classic study "Cavalcanti in Dante," in *Varianti e altra linguistica* (Torino: Einaudi, 1970), pp. 433–45, reprinted in *Un'idea di Dante: Saggi danteschi* (Torino: Einaudi, 1976), pp. 143–157.

15. See my Epilogue for a discussion of *Inferno* x.

16. The two Guidos seem to be Guinizelli and Cavalcanti, but Guido di Pino argues that they are Guittone and Guinizelli ("L'uno e l'altro Guido," *Ausonia* 23, nos. 2–3 [1968]:9–13). The deliberate ambiguity makes Dante's gesture all the more malicious. For an extensive bibliography of the scholarship generated by Dante's reference to the two Guidos, see Barolini, *Dante's Poets*, pp. 127–29.

17. Cf. Barolini, "Vergil: 'Poeta Fui,' " in *Dante's Poets*, pp. 201–256.

18. Calenda argues that the theme of impotence and psychic dissolution in Guido's poetry can be brought back to the concrete circumstance of the Republican triumph over, and castration of, the political power of the "magnate" families in Florence, which included of course the Cavalcanties. Calenda interprets the Guido-Dante relation in this key as well. With history and the future on the side of his triumphant class, Dante becomes a *synthetic*, that is to say appropriative, poet. With history and the future against *his* class, Guido becomes the poet of analysis, dissolution, and above all *expropriation* (*Per altezza d'ingegno*, pp. 98–118).

19. The point is made by Rachel Jacoff in "Poetry of Guido Cavalcanti." Editors usually refer us to Guido's *ballata* "Fresca rosa novella / piacente primavera," but as Jacoff notes, "since there is no other reference to the word *primavera* in *any* of Guido's extant lyrics I think this citation is one which is only possible because of the *Vita Nuova*. That is, it is Dante who creates the *senhal*" (p. 131).

20. Cf. Corti, *La felicità mentale*, pp. 3–37, esp. pp. 20–27.

21. Paolo Possiedi confirms that most of Guido's personifications

are metonymic and involve parts of the sentient self; see "Personifica-zione e allegoria nelle *Rime* di Guido Cavalcanti," *Italica* 52 (1975):37–49.

22. Rachel Jacoff, "Poetry of Guido Cavalcanti," p. 135.

5 The Death of Beatrice and the Petrarchan Alternative

1. Sanguineti, "Le visioni della *Vita Nuova*," *Ateneo Veneto*, Fac-simile speciale per il VII Centenario Dantesco, 1265–1965, (1965), p. 7.

2. For stylistic and structural perspectives on the poetic and pro-saic dimensions of the *libello*, see Michelangelo Picone, "Strutture poetiche e strutture prosastiche nella *Vita Nuova*." (Picone offers a pro-vocative reading of the episode of the "Ego tanquam centrum circuli" of chapter XII in terms of the relationship between poetry and prose). See also Vincent Moleta, "The *Vita Nuova* as a Lyric Narrative," *Fo-rum italicum* 12 (1978):369–90. In the same issue of *Forum italicum*, see Sara Sturm-Maddox, "The Pattern of Witness: Narrative Design in the *Vita Nuova*," pp. 216–32; for a more extended discussion of narra-tive design in the *Vita Nuova* see also Sturm-Maddox, *Petrarch's Meta-morphosis* (Columbia: University of Missouri Press, 1985), pp. 39–64. See also De Robertis, "L'idea del Libro," in *Il libro* (pp. 5–24). A monu-mental treatment of Dante's early prose is found in Aldo Vallone's *La prosa della "Vita Nuova."* Compare with Cecil Grayson's "Dante e la prosa volgare," in *Conque saggi danteschi* (Bologna: Pàtron, 1972), pp. 33–60.

3. Freud considers mourning and melancholia in relation to the phenomenon of narcissism, and we will see throughout the discussion of Petrarch the degree to which they intersect each other. See Sigmund Freud, "On Narcissism: An Introduction" (1914) and "Mourning and Melancholia" (1917), in *General Psychological Theory*, ed. Philip Rieff (New York: Macmillan, 1963), pp. 56–83 and 164–80.

4. Jacoff notes that while its idiom is Cavalcantian, the poem "completely takes over and reverses the meaning of Guido's lyric style, both in the detail of its psychologizing analysis and in the form of the poem" ("Poetry of Guido Cavalcanti," p. 161).

5. For a broader discussion of gender reversal in Dante, see Jef-frey Schnapp, "Dante's Sexual Solecisms: Genre and Gender in the *Commedia*" (forthcoming in *Romanic Review*).

6. J. E. Shaw "concluded" that to speak of Beatrice's death was

not in keeping with the purpose of the *libello* because, "owing to the suddenness and shocking character of the event, he had no memory of his own feelings on becoming aware of it" (*Essays*, p. 151).

7. The concept of shifters as a special class of signs that combine the dual function of symbol and index is developed by Roman Jakobson in *Shifters, Verbal Categories, and the Russian Verb*," in *Selected Writings*, 7 vols. (The Hague: Mouton, 1971), 2:130–47.

8. See Giorgio Agamben's discussion of the relation between shifters, voice, pronouns, and the here and now in *Il linguaggio e la morte* (Turin: Einaudi, 1982), pp. 28–34 and 43–51.

9. Compare this pattern with Benveniste's insight into the production of temporality in and through the moment of enunciation. Benveniste remarks that it is only in and through this moment that a concept of the present arises, and it is only through the concept of the present that a concept of time in general arises. "The present," he writes, "is properly the source of time. It is that presence in the world which only the act of enunciation makes possible, since (if we think about it) man has no other way of living the 'now' except by realizing it through the introduction of speech in the world" (*Problèmes de linguistique générale*, 2 vols. [Paris: Gallimard, 1974], 2:83 [my translation]). Unfortunately, it would require a whole study to reexamine the Petrarchan corpus from the perspective of Benveniste's linguistics and Jakobson's theory of shifters.

10. Although I am not persuaded by Sara Sturm-Maddox's thesis that the *Canzoniere* contains "the vestige of a narrative design" based on the *Vita Nuova*, I do agree that, were there such a design, it would constitute one of "the several strategies adopted by Petrarch to bridge the blank spaces between independent lyrics and to create the illusion of a chronological axis for his collection" (*Petrarch's Metamorphosis*, p. 42).

11. The *Canzoniere* is of course organized according to a chronological pattern, but as Robert Durling remarks in the superb introduction to his edition and translation of the anthology, "The work presents a *fictional* chronology that should not be confused with a real one, and the ordering of the poems derives from artistic principles" (*Petrarch's Lyric Poems*, trans. and ed. Robert Durling [Cambridge: Harvard University Press, 1976], p. 10). For a dicussion of Petrarch's resistance to the chronological ordering and representation of experience, see Paolo Rinucci "L'Amore tra natura e storia nella poesia del

Petrarca e nella lirica del Rinascimento," in *Convengo Internazionale Francesco Petrarca* (Rome: Accademia Nazionale dei Lincie, 1976), pp. 163–78. See also Bortolo Martinelli's extensive argument for how behind the *Canzoniere*'s apparently chronological order lies a principle of moral organization: *Petrarca e il Ventoso* (Rome: Minerva Italica, 1977), pp. 217–300. From another perspective, see Adolfo Jenni, "Un sistema del Petrarca nell'ordinamento del *Canzoniere*," *Studi in onore di Alberto Chiari*, 2 vols. (Brescia: Paideia, 1973), 2:721–37. Also, Thomas Roche, "The Calendrical Structure of Petrarch's *Canzoniere*," *Studies in Philology* 71 (1974):154–72.

12. See Durling's discussion of love and memory in Petrarch's *Canzoniere* (*Petrarch's Lyric Poems*, pp. 18–26).

13. I have followed Durling's prose translation but without dividing up the individual stanzas.

14. With regard to origins, utopia, and the grassy place as the place of a poetic quest, Giuseppe Mazzotta remarks, "In the hands of Petrarch, the language of the lyric is not the language of primary vision but its simulacrum, a secondary—prosaic, as it were—search for that original vision or its renewal." See Mazzotta, "Petrarch's Song 126," in *Textual Analysis: Some Readers Reading*, ed. Mary Ann Caws (New York: MLA, 1986), p. 130.

15. For a full account of Petrarch's different versions of his collection of vernacular poems see E. H. Wilkins, *The Making of the Canzoniere and Other Petrarchan Studies* (Rome: Edizioni di Storia e Letteratura, 1951).

16. Which by no means implies a stylistic equivalence. As William Kennedy notes, "By 'vario stile' one may understand the range of tones, moods, and attitudes that play off one another in balanced patterns of statement and reversal, thesis and antithesis, resolution and dissolution. The fourteen line structure beautifully captures such a varied evolution. . . . The 'vario stile' . . . characterizes the sonnet's aesthetic structure as well as the speaker's own *ethos*, his inner structure of thought throughout the collection of his poetry" (*Rhetorical Norms in Renaissance Literature* [New Haven: Yale University Press, 1978], pp. 26–27).

17. On the question of Augustine, Petrarch, and conversion, see John Freccero, "The Fig Tree and the Laurel: Petrarch's Poetics," *Diacritics* 5 (Spring 1975): 34–40. Also Nicolae Iliescu, *Il Canzoniere petrarchesco e Sant'Agostino* (Rome: Società accademica romena, 1962). See

also Sara Sturm-Maddox, "Augustine's Story: The Confessional Sub-text," in *Petrarch's Metamorphosis*, pp. 95-126.

18. The theme of the self's dispersion in Petrarch's poetry is the topic of Giuseppe Mazzotta's essay "The *Canzoniere* and the Language of the Self," *Studies in Philology* 75 (1978):271-296.

19. Cf. Kennedy, *Rhetorical Norms in Renaissance Literature*, pp. 20-25.

20. The bibliography surrounding the myth of Apollo and Daphne in the *Canzoniere* is extensive; some of the more recent and relevant studies include Marga Cottino-Jones, "The Myth of Apollo and Daphne in Petrarch's *Canzoniere*," in *Francis Petrarch, Six Centuries Later*, ed. Aldo Scaglione, Department of Romance Languages, University of North Carolina (Chapel Hill, 1975), pp. 152-76; Robert Durling, *Petrarch's Lyric Poems*, pp. 26-33, and "Petrarch's 'Giovane donna sotto un verde lauro,' " *Modern Language Notes*, 86 (1971):1-20; P. R. J. Hainsworth, "The Myth of Daphne in the *Rerum vulgarium fragmenta*," *Italian Studies* 34 (1979):28-44; Sara Sturm-Maddox, *Petrarch's Metamorphosis*, esp. chap. 2.

21. As for last words on Petrarch, the most beautiful, if not the most consonant with my own perception, come from Fredi Chiappelli's conclusion to his study of the language of Petrarch. In my own translation from the Italian:

> The existence of Laura—an incredible announcement of light, a promise of inexhaustible and perpetual comfort to existence. . . . The obstinate will to climb beyond the shadows and perceive a free and perpetual image; the energy that moves the whole fanciful, cultivated, and passionate man toward invention [*invenzione*] is a hard, adult energy, rooted in the maturity of character. It does not come from the system of imagination, nor from that of culture, nor from that of passion. It springs from the depths of experience, making its way and nourishing itself in passion, in culture, in the fantasy of the past, and it springs from the mute anguish of one who has since become aware of the inherent insufficiency of living. It is a conclusive anguish, for in no way has any aspect of existence shown that it could compensate [for the insufficiency]; if not the last resort of invention, which gives reality

to fugitive shadows, and which creates the virtue of wholeness in one, two, six diverse and complete fables that are neither confused nor inexplicit; and for an instant the invariable lightning from the palace of truth, having reached the summit of Atlantis, wins out over the imprecise and terrifying ghosts." (*Studi sul linguaggio del Petrarca: La Canzone delle visione* [Florence, 1971], pp. 228–29)

6 Beyond the Lyric

1. Paul Ricoeur, "Narrative Time," in *On Narrative*, ed. W. J. T. Mitchell (Chicago: University of Chicago Press, 1980), pp. 169, 170.

2. Singleton, *Essay*, p. 101.

3. The identity of the *donna gentile* has been an endless source of frustration for *dantisti*, since she reappears in the *Convivio* as an allegory for philosophy. In the later work Dante insists that she always was an allegory, but there is no such indication in the *Vita Nuova*. While some critics, like Bruno Nardi and J. E. Shaw, believe that she was born and died as an allegory, others, like Barbi, De Robertis, and Fausto Montinari, believe that she was in fact a real woman. After long reflection, I am persuaded that she was intended allegorically from the beginning but that later revisionary interventions on Dante's part have obscured the original story and left us with an insoluble enigma.

4. According to Barberi Squarotti, the new woman is a "terrestial image of Beatrice, a repetition of Beatrice, without the grace that was in Beatrice" ("Introduzione alla *Vita Nuova*," p. 53). Edmund G. Gardner relates the episode to Augustine's notion of *consuetudo carnalis* and says that it figures as "essentially what might be called a troubador version of the psychological situation described by Augustine." The situation in question is described by Augustine in Book VII of the *Confessions*, where he speaks of 'being dragged from Thee by mine own weight' " (See Gardner, *Dante and the Mystics*, p. 146).

5. The issue of mourning is a complex one in the *Vita Nuova*. From one perspective the work as a whole constitutes an "introjection," which Nicolas Abraham and Maria Torok have called the normal, as opposed to the deviant, work of mourning. In "introjection" a loss is made known publicly through acts that are essentially confes-

sional and discursive. Perhaps one could say that the *donna gentile* is nothing more than an agent of introjection, freeing discourse for the work of mourning, but such speculation, however potentially fruitful, takes us in another direction altogether. For Nicolas Abraham's and Maria Torok's post-Freudian theories of mourning and introjection, see *L'Ecorce et le noyau* (Paris: Flammarion, 1978), pp. 229–317.

6. Cf. Frank Kermode, *The Sense of an Ending: Studies in the Theory of Fiction* (Oxford: Oxford University Press, 1967); also Paul Ricouer, *Temps et récit*, vol. 1 (Paris: Edition du Seuil, 1983), and Gérard Genette, "Boundaries of Narrative," *New Literary History* 8, no. 1 (Autumn 1976):1–16.

7. The sedentary or immobile nature of the lyric disposition is dramatized by Dante in the wholly different context of *Purgatorio*. As Barolini points out, the epic poets—Virgil, Statius and Dante himself—are on the move, while the lyric poets in xxiv and xxvi are immobilized or trapped on their terraces. This difference—transit and stasis, or, eventually, epic and lyric—lies at the origin of the *libello*'s schizophrenic *prosimetrum* structure.

8. It was textual indications of passivity like these that led Mark Musa to argue that the author of the *Vita Nuova* submits its protagonist to a scathing critique, and that we are in no way to confuse this self-pitying, passive, and somewhat despicable character with the mature Dante who composed the work ("Essay on the *Vita Nuova*," pp. 168–74). A similar argument was first proposed by Jefferson Fletcher in "The 'True Meaning' of Dante's *Vita Nuova*," *Romanic Review* xi, no. 2 (1920):95–148. I find that both Musa and Fletcher exaggerate the case.

9. Robert Klein, "Spirito Peregrino." For the English translation see Robert Klein, *Form and Meaning*, trans. Madeline Jay and Leon Wieseltier (New York: Viking Press, 1979), pp. 62–88. Giorgio Agamben follows Klein's approach by rigorously reconstructing and integrating the various strands of medieval doctrines of the spirit; for his discussion of "Oltre la spera" in terms of pneumaphantasmology, see *Stanze: La parola e il fantasma nella cultura occidentale*, pp. 121–22.

10. In much stilnovist poetry the *spiriti* are depicted leaving the poet's eyes and rushing toward the lady to return to their subject with a visual imprint of the object of perception. Cavalcanti especially dramatizes the process of perception in terms of the *spirito visivo*'s journeys to and from the lady. Dante also personifies the spirit in this manner (see chapter xiv). Robert Klein demonstrates the extent to which

the *spirito visivo* functions as a subtle, almost dematerialized, *veil* that receives imprints and bears images across space. Dante's *spirito peregrino*, which is actually a sigh and therefore not, technically speaking, a *spirito visivo*, nevertheless operates as a *spirito visivo* in its departure from, and return to, the person. In its peregrination it literally *sees* Beatrice in heaven ("vede un donna") and returns to earth with an imprint of the image, as on a veil.

7 The Narrative Breakthrough

1. Paul Ricoeur, *Temps et récit*, 1:105 (my translation).

2. The term is used by L. Golden and O. B. Hardison in *Aristotle's Poetics: A Translation and Commentary for Students of Literature* (Englewood Cliffs, N.J.: Prentice Hall, 1968), p. 236.

3. Robert Hollander expresses a beautiful insight in the following manner:

> If we had nothing else, the two little verbs that tell us
> Beatrice's condition and activity in Paradise—she knows and
> she gazes—are really enough to let the major fact about her be
> a most salient one. . . . In the first twenty-seven chapters of
> the *Vita Nuova* Beatrice is described in the "historical
> past," that is, by the past absolute. In the next fourteen
> chapters Dante looks back to the dead Beatrice in the same
> tense. After the *mirabile visione* a small grammatical miracle
> not only resurrects her from the dead, it even stands as a re-
> buke to the backward-looking intention of the *libello*. . . . His
> new life can be said to be truly undertaken once he
> can speak of Beatrice in the present. ("Dante's Perceptions
> of Beatrice," *Dante Studies* 92 [1974]:11)

4. Louis O. Mink, "Interpretation and Narrative Understanding," *Journal of Philosophy* 69, no. 20 (1972):735–37.

5. This is what Arthur Danto, in his reflections on narrative and history, calls "the retroactive realignment of the past" (*Analytic Philosophy of History* [Cambridge: Cambridge University Press, 1965], p. 168).

6. "If a previous event is not significant with regards to an ulterior event in a story, it does not belong to that story" (ibid., p. 134). This principle of "consequential significance," as Danto calls it, describes what Dante means by *sentenzia*.

7. Cf. Frank Kermode, *The Sense of an Ending*.

8. Sanguineti observes with regard to the last chapter: "It is clear, therefore, that what falls into crisis for Dante is not really an idea of the lyric, the myth of the 'new rhymes,' or the doctrine of praise, but rather the idea of lyric itself, absolutely" ("Per una lettura," p. xliii). While I agree enthusiastically with Sanguineti, I am suggesting that the *Vita Nuova* is more than merely an immanent critique of the lyric insofar as the narrative prose embodies a positive alternative beyond the lyric.

9. Cf. John Freccero, "Medusa: The Letter and the Spirit" (*Dante's Poetics of Conversion*, pp. 119–35).

10. Cf. chapter 1, note 20.

8 Vision and Revision: The Provisional Essence of the *Vita Nuova*

1. Pietrobono, *Il poema sacro* (Bologna: Zanichelli, 1915); for his revised version of the theory see "Il rifacimento della *Vita Nuova* e le due fasi del pensiero dantesco," in *Saggi danteschi* (Torino, 1936), pp. 25–98.

2. This is the rubric of the last section of her *La felicità mentale: Nuove prospettive per Cavalcanti e Dante* (Torino: Einaudi, 1983), pp. 146–55.

3. Wanting to clear up the confusion, Salvatore Santangelo tried to find ambiguity in Dante's astronomical dating with the following suggestion: Although one revolution of the planet Venus is equivalent to 584 days in the Alfraganus system (hence twice those many days had passed, according to Dante's indication), there may have been some misinformation on Dante's part. Santangelo pointed out that Dante's son, Jacopo, using wrong astronomical information that he derived from Brunetto Latini's *Tresor*, estimated one revolution of Venus as equivalent to 291 days. Was Dante operating under the same error in the *Convivio*? A problem, ultimately, of dissemination, which Derrida defines as "ce qui ne revient pas au père." See S. Santangleo, "La composizione della *Vita Nuova*," *Saggi danteschi* (Padova, 1959), pp. 27 ff.

4. Maria Corti has shown conclusively that if Dante intended the word *fine* in a loose sense here, it is the *only* such usage throughout his works. See *La felicità mentale*, pp. 151–52.

5. The position of those who believe that she was intended alle-

gorically from the beginning, for example, Bruno Nardi and James E. Shaw, is challenged by De Robertis in "Il libro della *Vita Nuova* e il libro del *Convivio*," *Studi urbinati* 25 (1951):5–27. While Nardi advocated the *rifacimento* theory, J. E. Shaw rejected it early on through an elaborate attempt to date the first *canzone* of the *Convivio*. Shaw in fact devotes an entire (outdated) chapter on dating the *Vita Nuova*; see "The Date of the *Vita Nuova*," in *Essays*, pp. 1–51.

6. Michele Barbi, "La data della *Vita Nuova* e i primi germi della *Commedia*," in *Problemi di critica dantesca*, 2 vols. (Firenze: Sansoni, 1934) 1:99–112.; also idem, "Razionalismo e misticismo in Dante," *Studi danteschi* 17, no. 21 (1933): esp. 25–26; reprinted in *Problemi di critica dantesca*, 2:1–86.

7. An interview with Michele Barbi by P. Chistoni, *La seconda fase del pensiero dantesco: periodo degli studi sui classici e filosofi antichi e sugli espositori medievali* (Livorno, 1903), in *Bulletino della Società Dantesca Italiana*, n.s. 10, p. 316 (my translation).

8. Bruno Nardi, "S'ha da credere a Dante o ai suoi critici?" *Cultura Neolatina* 2 (1942):327–33.

9. "Non si vuole assolutamente qui entrare nella polemica Barbi-Nardi e men che meno nell'altra più colorita Barbi-Pietrobono, per carità; anche se il loro darsi a più riprese reciprocamente dell'ottuso nell'atto in cui si apostravano 'egregio dantista,' sia un rito culturale che può avere il suo fascino, quello delle cose da tempo perdute" (Maria Corti, *La felicità mentale*, p. 148).

10. Mario Marti, "Vita e morte della presunta doppia redazione della *Vita Nuova*," in *Studi in onore di Alfredo Schiaffini*, 2 vols. (Rome: Edizione dell'Ateneo, 1965), 2:657–69.

11. Corti, *La felicità mentale*, pp. 150–51 (my translation).

12. Colin Hardie's essay "Dante's 'Mirabile Visione': *Vita Nuova* XLII" (in *The World of Dante*, ed. Cecil Grayson [Oxford: Oxford University Press, 1980], pp. 123–45) neatly allegorizes this compulsion in the scholarship. In his preoccupation with the links between the miraculous vision and Dante's later works, he actually *forgets to read* the last chapter.

Epilogue

1. "And although such a claim runs counter to most of our present assumptions, the effort to formulate a convincing 'tale of the

tribe' still seems an undertaking of enormous value, one central not only to the continuing authority of verse, but to the very possibility of making sense of the conditions of our common history. . . . And then went down to the ship" (Michael Bernstein, *The Tale of the Tribe: Ezra Pound and the Modern Verse Epic* [Princeton: Princeton University Press, 1980], pp. 281–82).

2. "Whatever may have been his starting point, Dante evolved, as guardian of his Eden and personification of its spirit, a lovely girlish form, one of his prettiest conceptions. Such a figure had always haunted his fancy; it lurks in nearly all his lyric verse, whether dedicated to Beatrice, to the Donna Pietosa, to Philosophy, or to the unknown lady of the Casentino. In her solitude, her joyousness, her amorous song, her association with birds and flowers, Matelda belongs to the pastoral type" (from *La Divine Commedia*, ed. and annotated by C. H. Grandgent, revised by Charles S. Singleton [Cambridge: Harvard University Press, 1972], p. 562).

3. Michel Foucault, introduction and notes to Ludwig Binswanger's *Le rêve et l'existence* (Bruges: Desclée de Brower, 1954), p. 126 (my translation).

4. "Forse cui Guido vostro ebbe a disdegno" (*Inferno* x, 1. 64). I am not persuaded by the uneasy consensus among Italian *dantisti* that the *cui* must be read as a dative referring either to Beatrice or to God and not to Virgil (see Gianfranco Contini, *Poeti del Duecento*, 2:489. I am more persuaded by Singleton, who claims that the *cui* must be read "as a relative pronoun, direct object of a verb, and with a touch of the interrogative *chi* about it" ("*Inferno* x: Guido's Disdain," *Modern Language Notes* 77N (1962): 60). The question of Guido's "disdain" has generated much discussion and controversy. In addition to Favati's bibliography in his edition of the *Rime*, Marti's review in the entry for Cavalcanti in the *Enciclopedia dantesca*, and Singleton's bibliographical summary in "*Inferno* x: Guido's Disdain" (pp. 63–65), see Paolo Cherchi, "Il disdegno per Guido: una proposta," *L'Alighieri* 2 (1970):73–78, in which Cherchi suggests (tentatively) that it is Beatrice who disdains Guido and not the other way around.

5. See Ulrich Leo, "The Unfinished *Convivio* and Dante's Rereading of the *Aeneid*," *Medieval Studies* 13 (1951):41–64.

Index of Passages Cited

General Index

Abraham, Nicolas, 195n
Absolute present. *See* Eternal
  present
Accident, 55, 86
Agamben, Giorgio, 53, 183n,
  187n, 192n
Allegory, 60, 141–42
American Dante criticism, 1–4
Angiolieri, Cecco, 148
Anthology, idea of, 101, 104–5
Aquinas, 38–42, 173n, 179n, 180n,
  182n
Arete, 34
Aristotle, 101, 182n
Augustine, 195n
Authentic representation, 126–
  28
Averroism, 74, 87, 169, 188n

Baldelli, Ignazio, 183n, 185n
Barbi, Michele, 147–48, 182n,
  199n
Barolini, Teodolinda, 176–77n,
  190n, 196n
Beatitude, 135
Beatrice: as author, 65, 67; beatitude of, 135; beauty of, 40; as
  Christ figure, 48–49; and
  Giovanna, 88–89; greeting
  (passage) of, 21–22, 138; hypostasis of, 49–51; phenomenal/
  noumenal presence of, 19, 29,

48–49, 61, 126–27, 142–43; return after death in vision, 118;
return in earthly paradise, 163–
64. *See also* Body of Beatrice;
Death of Beatrice
Benveniste, 192n
Bernard, Saint, 11
Bernstein, Michael, 200n
Bigi, Emilio, 177n
Bird, Otto, 189n
Boccaccio, 63, 183n
Body of Beatrice: legitimation of
figurative language, 59; otherness of, 52–53; phenomenal/
noumenal presence, 19, 29, 48–
49, 61, 126–28, 142–43; resistance to allegory, 60; and
time, 142–43; versus attire, 22–
24, 28–29. *See also* Veil; Veil/
body
Boethius, 146, 182n
Bonagiunta: in *Purgatorio*, 31–33,
45; sonnet to Guido Guinizelli,
33
Bonfils Templer, Margherita de,
173n, 175n
Boyde, Patrick, 182n, 185n
Brophy, Anthony, 178n

Calenda, Corrada, 187–90n
Canzoniere (Petrarch), 100–109;
annual cycle of, 102, 169; as

About the Author

Robert Pogue Harrison is a member of the faculty of the Department of French and Italian at Stanford University. He is the author of *The Murano Workshop*.